VICTIMS OF TERRORISM AND EXTREMISM

THE SHIA

IDENTITY. PERSECUTION. HORIZONS.

SAYYID RIYADH AL-HAKEEM

Author: Sayyid Riyadh Al-Hakeem

Translator: Elvana Hammoud

Al-Hakeem, Riyadh, 1958

The Shia: Identity. Persecution. Horizons. – 1ˢᵗ ed.

ISBN: 978-0-692-39029-0

In the Name of Allah, the All-compassionate, the All-merciful

Praise belongs to God, the Lord of the Worlds

Peace and blessings be upon Your messengers and the last of Your prophets, Muhammad and his pure progeny

In dedication to those who have given us all
and asked for nothing in return

Table of Contents

Foreword

By Dr. Hassan Abbas

As the world grapples with religious extremism and consequent violence in the world of Islam, Sayyid Riyadh Al-Hakeem provides us a valuable opportunity to understand the political dynamics and theological debates within Islam. I had the privilege to have a long conversation with Sayyid in 2014 in Najaf focusing on the developments in the Muslim world. I was struck by his scholarly demeanor, thoughtful approach and creative thinking geared towards peaceful resolutions to the challenges faced by humanity today.

The Shia: Identity. Persecution. Horizons. is a penetrating historical account about Shia Muslims, enlightening us about their genesis, their struggles and most importantly their contribution to the Islamic faith. Unlike many similar efforts, this book is not a chronicle of Shia–Sunni rivalries. The book is more focused on what the author believes to be the essence and spirit of Islam. He intelligently differentiates between issues that are linked to Muslim identity and others that are more profound in terms of foundations of faith. Sayyid Al-Hakeem, an accomplished scholar and jurist, is not only well qualified to teach us about this subject but his access to the corridors of learning and education in the Holy City of Najaf makes him among the most ideal people to undertake this task.

Sayyid Al-Hakeem introduces the book with an explanation of the principles of Islam adhered to and pursued by the Shia as taught by the Prophet Muhammad and his family. The book is written in a fashion that makes it accessible to all aspiring to acquire knowledge on the subject. It is written in a simple and straightforward fashion. The author's primary goal is to clearly present the basic facts without delving into more complicated and contested theological arguments. It explains all the central features of faith as understood and practiced by Shia Muslims ranging from the concept of Prophethood & Imamate to a variety of rituals. It presents brief but very useful profiles of the 12 Imams revered especially by the Shia. In addition, it serves as an introduction to how scholarly traditions amongst the Shia were institutionalized despite seemingly insurmountable obstacles. He also wisely separates the spiritual aspects from the political matters.

The second half of the book briefly outlines the rich history of Shia Muslims as a people and a vibrant culture. The Shia Muslim community has spanned not only the Middle East and modern-day South Asia but various other parts of the world as well. The author then directs his efforts towards exposing the anti-Shia political hostilities in a historical context. He brings their story to the present by scrutinizing their current expressions that are obvious in the shape of current power struggles across the Muslim world. He deserves credit for providing a concise and credible historical account of how various Muslim rulers and regimes targeted sacred places of Islam revered by Shia Muslims in a systematic and coordinated fashion. It is a miracle that both Shia Muslims and their discourse have survived such tyranny and brutality. The passion of defiance against oppression and standing up to bigotry indeed has been the hallmark of Shia history. The Muslim dynasties that ruled over the Middle East for centuries knew well where the challenge to their dogmatism and autocracy could come from. Thus, a concerted effort to silence the Shia (as well as some other Muslim communities) reigned.

From the provocative Islamic revolution in Iran to the increasingly important role of Ayatollah Sistani and the religious establishment in Najaf, the consequences of the empowerment of Shia have varied. For the current power centers in Middle East, this 'Shia Revival' was seen as a challenge to their ways of governing. Globally, this is also seen as rebalancing the power inside the world of Islam. Shia population may be approximately 15 to 20 percent of the total Muslim population worldwide; however, in the Arab heartland it appears to be more of a 40/60 ratio. In relevant geopolitical and economic terms, Shia Muslims are mostly dominant in the oil producing regions of the Middle East.

This poignant and well-timed analysis of the Muslim dynamics brings great clarity to the complex series of events shaping the Muslim world today. It is a must read for both Muslim and non-Muslim audiences who are interested in understanding a Shia perspective that is written with the objective of pursuing inter-religious harmony and peaceful coexistence, encouraging tolerance and defeating sectarian agendas.

> **Professor Hassan Abbas** lives and teaches in Washington, D.C. and is author of 'The Taliban Revival: Violence and Extremism on the Pakistan-Afghanistan Frontier' (Yale University Press, 2014).

Introduction

In the name of Allah, the All-compassionate, the All-merciful

"O mankind! Indeed, We created you from a male and a female, and made you nations and tribes that you may identify yourselves with one another. Indeed the noblest of you in the sight of Allah is the most God wary among you. Indeed Allah is all-knowing, all-aware." (Quran, 49:13).

"Indeed those who have faith and do righteous deeds—it is they who are the best of men." (Quran, 98:7). In reference to faithful and righteous of this verse, The Prophet said to Imam Ali, "They are you and your Shia."[1]

Since the dawn of time, mankind has endured the tyranny of dictators and braved the consequences of discrimination and prejudice – be it religious, national, racial or ethnic. With the progression and advancement of humanity, culturally and economically, intellectuals projected the gradual decline of despotic regimes along with the discriminative policies orchestrated

[1] Jame' Al-Bayan, Al-Tabari: 3:335.

by those in power. Nonetheless, genocide and terrorism have still prevailed to this day. Iraq is a particular example of being ravaged by such senseless oppression and tyranny.

The mass murder of innocent civilians carried out by Saddam Hussein's dictator regime and the extremist Salafist organizations that terrorized the Iraqi people since his fall are still vivid in the hearts of Muslims across the world. Oppressive movements like these, with the consideration of today's day and age, became a deep concern for all those affected in and outside the region. Discussions on religious extremism and combating terrorism have taken a front row seat in political, social, economic, and religious dialogue across the globe. Unfortunately, Islam is often the target of finger pointing by some pundits who are quick to associate the terrorists with the religion itself simply because the terrorists claim that their actions are in Islam's name.

In contrast, impartial observers have noted the resurgence of the Shia, specifically after the fall of Saddam's oppressive regime in Iraq. Despite a long history of suffering, oppression, and persecution prior to, during and after the fall of Saddam's brutal regime in 2003, judiciousness and moderation have remained prominent characteristics of the Shia jurists in Najaf, Iraq. The rise of Shia Islam has since become a hot topic of research and dialogue in various circles amongst researchers, intellectuals and think tanks. Thus, to add to this dialogue the idea for this book was born, to briefly introduce Shia Islam – its beliefs, culture and history – from three dimensions:

1. The Shia Identity
2. Persecution and Oppression
3. Prospects for the Future

In addition to this book serving as an introduction to Shia Islam, the reader should note several key points:

1. The existence of various schools of thought within Islam today is fundamentally due to differing views and understandings of the religion, its principles and its teachings, from its earliest days. This disparity is not limited to a few ritual practices; rather, there exist significant differences in some of the most foundational principles of Islam and its primary teachings. This reality was clearly evident during the Umayyad Empire, a dynasty that reigned for over a hundred years commencing only 50 years after the Prophet's death. Umayyad rule was responsible for many of the negative ramifications on various social and theological values integral to Islam. Moreover, it is misguided to burden Islam with the responsibility of the practices of a fringe element that proclaim themselves to be Muslim when their actions directly oppose the true teachings of Islam practiced by the overwhelming majority of Muslims around the world.

2. Shia, who represent a sizable portion of Muslims worldwide, have systematically been the victims of terrorism in all of the countries where terrorists are known to be active, most prominently Iraq, Pakistan and Afghanistan. The animosity terrorists hold against Shia started long before the clash of interests between Western countries and terrorist groups.

3. The suffering Shia endured through genocide and terrorism has been common not only in modern times but throughout history as well. Historically, Shia have long been subjected to campaigns of terrorism and genocide at the hands of ruthless rulers and extremist groups. This book will briefly touch on some of these cases.

4. Most genocidal practices have happened, and continue to happen, through the careful planning or initiation of

oppressors who do not adhere to any religion. Their tactics include compelling those in power and/or leveraging extremist groups to execute their plans. Today, terrorists are provided with great financial and logistical capabilities along with immense media coverage by oppressive dictator regimes pulling the necessary strings behind the scenes.[2]

5. The Shia's steadfastness in the face of persecution and genocidal campaigns is primarily due to the nature of their ideological and cultural foundation. These structures are built firmly on commonly held values such as patience, perseverance, discipline, logic, and above all, a culture of peaceful coexistence.

6. The independence of the Shia religious establishment, particularly in Najaf, from the influence of governments and dictatorships, despite the heavy price paid for that independence, is worthy of serious study. Such a study will help us learn and save religious institutions from the control of authoritarian regimes and their attempts to expedite their plans through those institutions in the name of the religion.

In conclusion, I pray that I have succeeded through this humble work towards the overall goal of the Quran, that of bringing nations and societies together. "O mankind! Indeed, We created you from a male and a female, and made you nations and tribes that you may identify yourselves with one another.

---

[2] This is not a speculative political analysis; rather it is based on tangible facts and official information that confirm the care and support of dictator governments to terrorist groups as was evident in Iraq since the fall of the oppressive regime in 1424 AH / 2003 AD. Oftentimes, the role of dictatorships in supporting terrorism becomes evident after their fall, as was the case in the role of the Hosni Mubarak regime in Egypt and Muammar Ghadaffi in Lybia. Further proof of the above was also in the conditions and the place of residence of Osama Bin Laden, near the Pakistani capital in an area under the control of the Pakistani army intelligence, which became known after his killing on the 28th of Jamadi Al-Thani, 1432 AH or May 2nd, 2011 AD.

Indeed the noblest of you in the sight of Allah is the most God wary among you. Indeed Allah is all-knowing, all-aware." (Quran, 49:13)

I pray for the day when truth, justice and peace reign.

Riyadh Al-Hakeem

3/29/1432 AH; 2/3/2011 AD

First Dimension
IDENTITY

The Identity of Shia

Who Are the Shia?

The word Shia in the Arabic language means "the followers." The world-renowned linguist Khalil ibn Ahmad Al-Farahidi said, "The Shia of a man are his companions and followers."[1]

Ibn Manthour said, "This name became prevalent for those who took Ali and the people of his household (peace upon them all) as their leaders until this became their special name. And so it became that if a person says so and so is a Shia, it would become known that he is one of them."[2]

This term is specifically in reference to the Twelver Shia, who believe in the twelve Imams (leaders) that came after Prophet Muhammad per his guidance. The first of the twelve Imams is Ali ibn Abi Talib and the last of them is Muhammad Al-

---

[1] Tarteeb Keetab Al-Ayn: 436.
[2] Leessan Al-Arab: 7/258.

Mahdi. Today, there are over 200 million Shia Muslims worldwide.

The Essence of Islam

It is typical for any intellectual or cultural system to gradually spawn a number of varied schools of interpretations and analysis. Religion is no exception in that regard. Various sects and groups came to be based on differences in positions and jurisprudence pertaining to the principles and teachings of religion. This phenomenon is also applicable to Islam, a religion established in the city of Medina by the Holy Prophet Muhammad, away from the oppression and pressures of his enemies. It is in the haven of Medina that he began completing his teachings so as to form a distinct and coherent intellectual, cultural and legislative system for the adherents of the religion.

It is worthy to note the differences in attitudes and visions that came to fruition in regards to Islamic teachings even during the Prophet's life. He warned of the growing rift amongst his followers. Such a rift was observed to be due to a number of reasons: trivial disputes, extremism, and personal and group interests. The Prophet emphasized the main principles on which Islam was founded – reason, moderation and human values. He told his people, "I was sent to perfect the best of ethics,"[3] and that the Quran describes the Islamic nation as, "a medium (just) nation." (Quran, 2:143)

This inherent understanding of Islam is best illustrated through the actions of Imam Ali who was appointed by Prophet Muhammad as the gateway to knowledge saying, "You will

---

[3] Al-Kafee: 2/99, Bab Hossson Al-Khalek.

reveal to my nation that which they will differ about after my time."[4]

Imam Ali was surrounded by many of the same senior companions that accompanied Prophet Muhammad. He influenced and inspired them to the point that they became known as Ali's Shia and followers; a fitting title for those who were the seed of Shia Islam. This quality was unique to the Shia school of thought. Thus, it reasonably follows that Shia Islam manifested the most fundamental and unadulterated path to realizing the teachings of Prophet Muhammad. Crystallized at the inception of the Islamic core in Medina, Imam Ali led the followers of Prophet Muhammad after his death. In his discourse on the Shia, Abu Hatem said, "…that was the title given to four companions: Abuthar, Ammar, Mokdad and Salman…"[5]

These were the closest companions of the Prophet and they were the most committed to his teachings. They followed Imam Ali, along with other loyal companions, becoming the first generation of Shia.

Several texts indicate that the title Shia was first used by the Prophet himself to describe Ali's companions, including a narration by ibn Barzah saying, "the Prophet recited, 'Indeed those who have faith and do righteous deeds—it is they who are the best of men.' (Quran, 98:7) He also said, 'that is you Ali and your Shia…'"[6]

---

[4] Al-Moustadrek ala Al-Saheehein: 926-929.

[5] Haweyat Al-Tashay': 27, as obtained from Keetab Al-Zeenah by Abi Hatem.

[6] Shawahed Al-Tanzeel, 2/464. Also Jame' Al-Bayan by Al-Tabari: 3/335. Fateh Al-Kadeer by Al-Shoukani: 5/477. Al-Neehaya fee Ghareeb Al-Hadeeth by ibn Al-Atheer, Madat Al-Kame': 4/160.

The companion Salman Al-Farsee said, "We pledged allegiance to the Messenger of God and to recognize Ali ibn[7] Abi Talib as our Imam and to pledge allegiance to him..."[8]

The most significant characteristics of Imam Ali and his companions are as follows:

1. Absolute faith in the principles of Islam. Such faith was evident in their selflessness, generosity, and readiness for sacrifice. Their character had no signs of weakness nor did they ever experience defeat.

2. Unwavering dedication and accord under the leadership of Prophet Muhammad, as reflected in their unconditional subordination to him that had no hint of objection or hesitation in carrying out his orders and directives.

3. Application of the moral and humanitarian dimensions of Islam and understanding the religion's focus on the human spirit in accordance with the Prophet's saying, "I was sent to perfect the best of ethics."[9] They understood that Islam is not merely a set of theoretical instructions and abstract worship rituals, nor is it a method for controlling and oppressing others.

    This was reflected in the lifestyle of Imam Ali and his companions. They lived in adherence to the principles of justice and humanity; removed from seeking position, power and privilege. These ethics were also manifested in Imam Ali's policies during his governance. He implemented public policies that reinforced social justice and moved to disintegrate a caste system that had

---

[7] *Ibn* is an Arabic word meaning "son of," followed by the individual's father's name, which was often used both in pre-Islamic and Islamic times as a means of identification – similar to the Western surname.

[8] Khotat Al-Sham: 5/251.

[9] Al-Kafee: 2/99, Bab Hossson Al-Khalek.

been created de facto in some aspects and de jure in others by previous rule.

4. A comprehensive understanding of the teachings of Islam, based on reason and moderation, removed from vanity, rigidity and extremism. We see this in what they left behind in their legacies of knowledge, society, politics, leadership, loyalty and courage.

The philosopher Henry Stubbe said of Imam Ali, "He had a contempt of the world, its glory and pomp, he feared God much, gave many alms, was just in all his actions, humble and affable; of an exceeding quick wit and of an ingenuity that was not common, he was exceedingly learned, not in those sciences that terminate in speculations but those which extend to practice."[10]

---

[10] An Account of the Rise and Progress of Mahometanism-With the Life of Mahomet, 1705, p. 83.

The Shia Doctrine

Shia doctrine is built on five fundamental principles: Monotheism, Divine Justice, Prophethood, Imamah[13], and the Day of Judgment.

First: Monotheism

Shia believe in one God – the Creator of the Universe, the Cause of all causes, the Giver of life and sustenance, the First and the Last, the One, the Independent who has no equal, no partner, or anything that is like Him. Beyond discussions of philosophical proofs to the oneness of God, or His unique existence for that matter, we need to look no further than what lies before our eyes to see that there must have been an artist to paint such a beautiful picture that is our world.

---

[13] Imamah is derived from the Arabic word Imam, which means leader. Imamah refers to the divine leadership after the Prophet. It is a belief essential to Shia doctrine, holding that God ordained leaders and successors to the Prophet Muhammad – the first of which was Imam Ali ibn Abi Talib.

It is worthy to note that Muslims often use the Arabic word *Allah* as the "name" of God. Allah in Arabic simply means "the God." Allah, God, is the same god of all the monotheistic faiths – the only difference is the language. Even within Islamic communities, Muslims do not always refer to God by the Arabic word – Allah. Persians say *Khuda*, Turks says *Tanrı*, and Americans say *God*. It is simply a matter of language.

Second: Divine Justice

God is the ever living. He is absolutely independent. Omnipotent. Omniscient. All wise. All kind. All merciful. Shia doctrine emphasizes the Divine Justice of God – that despite His absolute ability and because of His absolute perfection, no injustice can come from Him. Any incident of injustice is logically repulsive and thus cannot be attributed to God. This Shia principle is in contradiction to doctrine of justice within other schools of thought in Islam. A commonly held belief in other schools is that God is just in reality; however, it is His right to commit injustice. These other schools of thought believe that although He may commit injustice, He cannot be questioned about what He does. They have based this belief on their understanding of the Quranic verse, "He cannot be questioned concerning what He does and they shall be questioned." (Quran, 21:23). In contrast, the Shia interpret this verse to mean that God cannot be questioned because He is just and perfect; thus, His work cannot be incomplete, evil, or unjust. God is not subjected to a separate system of justice against which His actions are measured; rather, everything God does is just and thus justice is based on His actions and will. In addition, acts of injustice are characteristic of the oppressive and the oppressive are weak. God is the essence of perfection and virtue and cannot be tainted with such weakness or oppressiveness. This is not just a theoretical ideological distinction; it is a significant difference in creed that has practical implications on a person's worldview.

Third: Prophethood

Prophethood is the Muslim belief that God entrusted His worshippers, at different times, the burden and responsibility of carrying His message to their respective communities. God appointed His prophets to guide mankind and relay His message to humanity. The Shia believe in all of the divine prophets, the most prominent of whom are Prophets Noah, Abraham, Moses, Jesus and Muhammad (peace be upon them all).

The Shia also believe that to bear the responsibility of the Divine message, the prophets must be the exemplars of human perfection and must possess a range of characteristics, most notably:

1. **Courage**. The prophet must be courageous in order to stand in the face of hardship and adversity. The prophet has to be firm in the challenges that come his way, especially before tyrants and oppressive rulers. It would be unbecoming for a prophet of God to be cowardly when faced with threats, challenges and risks. Prophet Muhammad was an exemplar of courage and bravery. At the advent of his message, the tyrant pagans of Mecca tried whatever they could to stop his preaching and bring a halt to his movement. They demanded from the Prophet's uncle Abu Talib – the most prominent individual in Mecca who embraced the Prophet and constantly came to his defense – that he forbids Muhammad from preaching his message. When Abu Talib told his nephew of their unfettered lobbying, the Prophet said, "O Uncle, by God, if they put the sun in my right

hand and the moon in my left so that I abandon [the Message], I would never do so."[14]

2. **Honesty**. One of the most essential characteristics of the holder of God's message is honesty. If a prophet of God ever lied, it would draw the possibility that he could lie to the people regarding the content of revelation. On another level, if his people thought him to be dishonest they would doubt the message that he carried. Thus, the prophet of God must be highly regarded for his honesty amongst his people. In addition, he must be an individual who has never lied to ensure that the delivery of God's message is unadulterated.

3. **Integrity**. In addition to honesty, God's prophets have to be individuals who embody the highest level of integrity. This is to further ensure that God's message is delivered in a complete manner without manipulation or change. An individual with true integrity will not betray the divine responsibility assigned to him. Prophet Muhammad was known for his integrity even before he was assigned to deliver God's message; and that is why he was praised as "the Trusted" and "the Honest."[15] The people of Mecca entrusted him with their possessions and continued to trust and confide in him even after he declared his message. He was the most trusted amongst the people despite their differences with his doctrine and their enmity towards him during the thirteen years he was in Mecca. When he emigrated from Mecca to Medina, situated about 420 km away, he ordered Ali ibn Abi Talib to return these trusts to their owners and so he did.[16] This act alone reflects the ex-

---

[14] Al-Seera Al-Nabaweeyah by Ibn Hesham: 1/302.
[15] Al-Fada'el: 80.
[16] Amta' Al-Asma' by Al-Makreezee: 38.

tent of his integrity, that he would honor the trusts and promises he made even to those who wished him dead.

4. **Role Model.** As the prophet of God, the people will look to him for guidance and leadership. Guidance is more than words and speech. People are inspired by the example of their leader. Thus, as the representative of God, the prophet must be the people's role model and the best possible example for them. If he were to be anything other than that, he would be inadvertently permitting his followers to fall short of honoring God's laws and commands. If the prophet is not an exemplar for the people, his word is of no weight. If he does not do everything that God has commanded the people to do and abstain from everything that God has prohibited, then why would the people take him as their divine leader? The Quran addresses the role of the Prophet to the people in the verse, "O Prophet! surely We have sent you as a witness, and as a bearer of good news and as a warner, And as one inviting to Allah by His permission, and as a light-giving torch." (Quran, 33:45-46) As the light-giving torch, the prophet shows the people the way with his good example.

In addition, Shia doctrine holds that Islam, as the last of the monotheistic religions, focuses on the following:

1. Balance. The balance between humanity's spiritual and material dimensions and their respective needs without neglecting either one. Just as physical instincts are not to be given free reign, there is also an aversion to monasticism and the forbidding of permissible fun as God Almighty says, "Say: Who has prohibited the embellishment of Allah which He has brought forth for His servants and the good provisions?" (Quran, 7:32)

2. Moderation and Tolerance. The doctrine emphasizes moderation and tolerance and thus renounces militancy and extremism. The Prophet said, "I brought you an easy and forgiving doctrine."[17]

3. Morals and Ethics. Islam is a religion based on ethics. Harmony between human beings comes from treating one another with honor, dignity and respect. The prophets of God established these ethics as a fundamental objective of faith, emphasizing that people hold on to their values and morals. The Prophet of Islam said, "I was sent to perfect the best of ethics."[18] That is exactly what he did. He manifested the highest levels of virtue through his impeccable character and conduct, whereby even his enemies knew him to be the most trustworthy and honest man of Arabia.

4. Reason. The fundamentals of Shia creed are not only built upon divine principles but can be entirely derived from pure reason without reference to religious text. Furthermore, the principles of Shia Islam work harmoniously with diverse societies and cultures. The faith does not enfranchise rigidity and stagnation; instead it fosters growth and progress. In a narration from Imam Jaafar Al-Sadiq (the sixth Imam), "The Quran is alive and does not die. It continues just like the day and the night and just like the sun and the moon. And it applies at our end just like it applied at our beginning."[19]

5. Just Governance. Any individual who assumes a role of governance or leadership must be just and of high moral character. Leaders and governors bear the responsibility

---

[17] Al-Naseereyat: 46.
[18] Al-Kafee: 2/99 Bab Hossson Al-Khalek.
[19] Tafseer Al-Ayashee: 2/219.

of applying social justice and promoting the advancement and prosperity of the community.

Fourth: Imamah

Prophet Muhammad did not leave the nation without guidance but rather he appointed an Imam, i.e. a leader, to succeed him. This appointment was ordained by God, emphasized throughout the Prophet's life and sealed with an epic proclamation at Ghadeer Khum in 10 AH / 632 AD.

Just like Prophet Abraham left the nation in the hands of his descendants, so did Prophet Muhammad. This is why Muslims tie together the blessings upon Prophet Abraham and his progeny to blessings upon Muhammad and his progeny. They say, "O' Allah, bless Muhammad and the family of Muhammad just like you blessed Abraham and the family of Abraham; you are Merciful and Glorified."[20] The twelve Imams after the Prophet were all from his progeny; however, they were not selected out of nepotism or to form a Muhammadan dynasty.

The Imams were chosen because they were the most deserving and best fit to carry the torch of divine leadership after the Prophet. Each of the Imams, beginning with Imam Ali ibn Abi Talib, manifested the pinnacle of morality, ethics, knowledge, wisdom, and leadership. Their relation to the Prophet was indeed an honor, but it was not the reason for their leadership. This is similarly held in regards to our prophets throughout history and their relationships with their relatives. Jacob had many sons, but it wasn't any of them that held the torch of prophethood after him – it was only Joseph. Aaron led the children of Israel alongside Moses, not because he was

---

[20] Fayd Al-Kadeer: 2/608.

Moses' brother but because he was the most pious, honorable, able and devoted individual – second only to Moses himself.

Up until his last day on Earth, Prophet Muhammad emphasized to his followers to hold on to the Quran and their relationship with Ahlulbayt, his family. It became a famous Islamic tradition, known as Hadith Al-Thaqalayn, "Verily, I am leaving among you two precious things (*thaqalayn*): the Book of God and my kindred (`*itrah*), my household (*Ahlulbayt*); for indeed, the two will never separate until they come back to me by the Pond [of *al-Kawthar* on the Day of Judgment]."[21] This narration has been cited by numerous narrators and on a number of occasions, the most relevant being Ghadeer Khum.

Upon the Prophet's return to Medina from his Farewell Pilgrimage to Mecca, he stopped in an area called Ghadeer Khum. He ordered the Muslims to set up a pulpit so that he may address the thousands that had been with him on his last pilgrimage. The thousands of Muslims gathered and the Prophet ascended the pulpit made of stacked stones, saddles and cloth. He asked the thousands present, "Who has more authority over the believers than they do over themselves." The masses roared in unison, "It is you O' Messenger of God!" Ali was standing next to the Prophet, as he always was. The Prophet grabbed Ali's arm and raised it high so that the thousands could see and said, "Whoever I am his Master, Ali is his Master."[22]

This proclamation did not come as a shock to the Muslims, because from the onset of Islam to his very last day the Prophet repeatedly described Ali as his brother, trustee, successor and vicegerent. Heavily narrated in both major schools of thought,

---

[21] Masnad Ahmad: volume 3/14, 17, 26, 59. Sunan Al-Tarmadhi: 5/329, Ketab Al-Manakeb (21) chapter on Manakeb Imam Ali ibn Abi Talib (as), narration 2724.

[22] Al-Sawaek Al-Mohreka: 42, as reported from Al-Tirmadhi, Al-Neesa'ee and Ahmad.

the Prophet said, "This affair [Islam] shall neither pass nor will come to an end while my twelve successor pass in it. All of them will be from Quraysh."[23]

The Twelve Successors are:

1. Imam Ali ibn Abi Talib
2. Imam Hassan ibn Ali
3. Imam Hussain ibn Ali
4. Imam Ali Zayn Al-Abideen
5. Imam Muhammad Al-Baqir
6. Imam Jaafar Al-Sadiq
7. Imam Moussa Al-Kadhim
8. Imam Ali Al-Rida
9. Imam Muhammad Al-Jawad
10. Imam Ali Al-Hadi
11. Imam Hassan Al-Askari
12. Imam Muhammad Al-Mahdi (*The Awaited One*)

Ali ibn Abi Talib

(23 BH - 40 AH[24] / 598 – 661 AD)

Ali was born on the 13th of Rajab 25 BH (598 AD) to Abu Talib and Fatima bint[25] Asad. When the pangs of labor began, Ali's mother was near the Holy Kaaba. During the pain she endured Fatima gravitated towards the House of God. She held onto the walls of the Kaaba as the pain increased. After a few moments, the walls of the Kaaba miraculously began to open up before her. The brick and rock tore asunder, creating a

---

[23] Al-Mo'jam Al-Kabeer, Vol. 2, pg 285, Tr. No. 2068 and 2069; Sahih Al-Muslim, Kitab Al-Imaarah; Kefaayah Al-Asar, pg 51, Chap 6, Tr. No. 3; Al-Khesaal, pg 469-473. Tr. No 12-30; Mukhtasar Al-sahih Al-Muslim by Tirmidhi, Tr. No. 1196.

[24] AH is the abbreviation for "After Hijra." Hijra refers to the Prophet Muhammad's migration from Mecca to Medina in 622 AD – the beginning of the Islamic calendar.

[25] The word *bint* is the female variant of *ibn*. Bint means "daughter of."

space for her to enter. The walls closed back up behind her. She gave birth to her newborn son Ali, being the first and only individual to be ever born in the Holy Kaaba. Our narrations say that Fatima stayed in the Kaaba for three days with her newborn son. When the walls opened up again, by God's will, Fatima calmly walked out as she gently held her newborn on her arm mesmerized by the beauty of her child. Her family was waiting outside the walls of the Kaaba, ready to greet her and the new addition to the family. As she walked out, there stood her husband Abu Talib and Abu Talib's nephew, Muhammad. They were overcome with beaming smiles and laughter of joy as Fatima graced them with the newborn Ali. Muhammad would ask to hold Ali in his arms and embrace his baby cousin. As Muhammad cradled the newborn in his arms, Ali opened his eyes and Muhammad would be the first sight that Ali would see.

When Ali was only about five years old, a famine hit metropolitan Mecca. Abu Talib had a large family and it became increasingly difficult to provide for the entire family and ensure that every one of his children was taken care of. Muhammad told Abu Talib that he would like to take his younger cousin Ali into his home to raise him and alleviate Abu Talib's worries. Abu Talib agreed and thanked Muhammad for his honorable gesture, as he was confident that his son would be in the best of hands with Muhammad. He surely was.

Ali grew up in the house of Muhammad as a younger brother. Ali followed Muhammad wherever he went, accompanying him like a shadow. What Muhammad did, Ali would do the same. As a young man, Ali's character and conduct became a mirrored reflection of Muhammad.

When Ali was twelve years old, Muhammad declared his message. Muhammad's loyal wife Khadija was the first individual to accept his message and become a follower of Islam. Despite his youth, Ali showed the greatest display of maturity, courage and loyalty to Muhammad by becoming the first male to follow him. As the student and disciple of Muhammad, Ali was one of the few who accepted Islam without ever previously worshipping other than God. Because he did not bow down or worship anyone other than God, in his youth or adulthood, Muslims from all schools of thought say "*karamallahu wajhah*" (may God honor his face) when they refer to Ali.

According to well-known historical accounts of Al-Tabari and Ibn Athir, Muhammad invited his near of kin comprised mostly of his uncles and cousins to a feast. This invitation became known as "Da'wat Al-Asheera" – the Invitation of the Near of Kin. At the feast, Muhammad announced his prophethood, his message and movement. He said that whoever assisted him in his call to faith would become his brother, trustee, successor and vicegerent. This was not just an invitation to break bread; it was an invitation to support the Message of God. Of those who were present, only Ali stepped forward to answer the call. Though the youngest amongst them, Ali stood confident and stated, "I will support you O' Messenger of God." The prophet nodded and smiled at the courageous Ali. Still, he repeated the invitation three times, and every time Ali was the only person to stand and answer Muhammad. It was as if the prophet repeated the invitation, not expecting that someone else would respond but to reaffirm Ali's position in the minds of those present. Ali's persistence was met with Muhammad's contentment; and thus, Muhammad declared that Ali was his brother, trustee, successor and vicegerent.

For the thirteen years the Prophet spent in Mecca, Ali was his closest supporter, companion and defender. Nonetheless, pressure and danger from the chieftains of Mecca continued to grow as the Prophet's popularity flourished. A time came where an assassination threat on the Prophet's life was imminent, and thus, Muhammad planned to migrate to Medina to escape harm. The assassination plot was to be carried out while Muhammad was asleep in his home. So, Ali risked his own life by sleeping in Muhammad's cot to lead the assassins to believe that Muhammad was still home. When they snuck into the house to carry out their assassination, Ali rose from the sheets sword in hand ready to fight and defend the honor of the Prophet. The assassins were shocked and scattered out of the house as their plot had failed. In the meantime, the Prophet was able to ride into safety's hands as he approached Medina.

Ali's moments of bravery and loyalty are too many to mention in this short account of his life. He was the champion of the battlefield and the temple. He was the hero of Badr, Uhud, Khaybar, Hunayn, and every battle that was waged on the Prophet; yet, he was the most serene in his prayers and supplication. He was firm but kind. He was confident but humble. He was a leader and a servant. He manifested every feature and characteristic of a true follower of Muhammad. Not only was Ali the Prophet's closest companion, trustee, vicegerent and successor, he was the only man to have the honor of fathering the grandchildren of Muhammad. By divine grace and order, Muhammad married his only daughter – Lady Fatima – to Ali. Their children, Hassan and Hussain, were so dear to the Prophet that he addressed them as his own sons. Until the Prophet's dying day, Ali brought happiness, confidence, and contentment to the heart of the Prophet.

Ali was the most salient example of a just leader. He was keen to public affairs, giving unprecedented attention to the poor and needy. Even when Ali was Caliph, he would visit the homes of orphaned children to give them food and gifts. For his unwavering dedication and commitment to them, he became known as the 'Father of the Orphans.'

Ali was merciful and tolerant even to his opponents and those who did not pledge allegiance to him or recognize his governance. He said, "I accept whoever pledges allegiance to me and I release whoever refuses."[26]

For thirty years after the Prophet's death, Ali did not wage war or label those who opposed him as heretics, including the militants that waged war on him known as the *Khawarij*[27]. His words were famous in their regard when he said, "I have but three promises. As long as you are with us, we will not keep you from God's mosques if you invoke His name therein. We will not deny you peace as long as you live with us in peace. We will not fight you unless you fight us."[28] When asked about those that fought him he would say, "they are our brothers and they have wronged us."[29] His strength was beyond overpowering those that stood against him. He was more concerned with protecting the nation of Muhammad and the faith of Islam than defending his own rights and status.

The lessons and teachings of Imam Ali continue to inspire people to this very day. In the Arab Human Development Report 2002[30], "Creating Opportunities for Future Generations"

---

[26] Al-Imamah wa Al-Seeyassah: 1/176.

[27] The event of Tahkeem gave rise to the Khawarij, a group of Muslims who believed that both Ali ibn Abi Talib and Muawiya should be removed because their decision to appoint arbiters to decide the dispute went against established tradition. The Khawarij amassed an army and prepared to attack Ali ibn Abi Talib. The armies met at Nahrawan in modern day Iraq. Although Ali ibn Abi Talib was victorious in the battle, the remnants of the Khawarij would continue to cause trouble and would ultimately succeed in assassinating Ali ibn Abi Talib.

[28] Tareekh Al-Tabari: 5/7.

[29] Wasa'el Al-Shia: 11/62.

[30] Review the text (addendum 2-4) issued by the Arab Human Development Report – The United Nations Development Program for the year 2002 AD and at the following website (both in English and Arabic):

Http://www.arab-bdr.org/publications/contents/arabic/2002/ahdr2002a.pdf

issued by the United Nations Development Program, the report shed light on the teachings of Imam Ali in relation to governance, knowledge and work.

The report chose the following sayings of Imam Ali ibn Abi Talib pertaining to his knowledge and work:

- No vessel is limitless, except for the vessel of knowledge, which forever expands.
- If God were to humiliate a human being, He would deny him knowledge.
- No wealth equals the mind, no poverty equals ignorance, no heritage equals culture, and no support is greater than advice.
- Wisdom is the believer's quest, to be sought everywhere, even among the deceitful.
- A person is worth what he excels at.
- No wealth can profit you more than the mind, no isolation can be more desolate than conceit, no policy can be wiser than prudence, no generosity can be better than decency, no heritage can be more bountiful than culture, no guidance can be truer than inspiration, no enterprise can be more successful than goodness, and no honor can surpass knowledge.
- Knowledge is superior to wealth. Knowledge guards you, whereas you guard wealth. Wealth decreases with expenditure, whereas knowledge multiplies with dissemination. A good material deed vanishes as the material resources behind it vanish, whereas to knowledge we are indebted forever. Thanks to knowledge, you command people's respect during your lifetime and kind memory after your death. Knowledge rules over wealth. Those who treasure wealth perish while they

Http://www.arab-bdr.org/publications/other/ahdr/ahdr2002e.pdf

are still alive, whereas scholars live forever; they only disappear in physical image, but in hearts, their memories are enshrined.

- Knowledge is the twin of action. He who is knowledgeable must act. Knowledge calls upon action; if answered, it will stay; otherwise, it will depart.

The following are quotes the report references from the words of Imam Ali ibn Abi Talib's on governance:

- He who has appointed himself an Imam of the people must begin by teaching himself before teaching others; his teaching of others must be first by setting an example rather than with words for he who begins by teaching and educating himself is more worthy of respect than he who teaches and educates others.

- Your concern with developing the land should be greater than your concern with collecting taxes, for the latter can only be obtained by developing whereas he who seeks revenue without development destroys the country and the people.

- Seek the company of the learned and the wise in search of solving the problems of your country and the righteousness of your people.

- No good can come in keeping silent as to government or in speaking out of ignorance.

- The righteous are men of virtue, whose logic is straightforward, whose dress is unostentatious, whose path is modest, whose actions are many and who are undeterred by difficulties.

- Choose the best among your people to administer justice among them. Choose someone who does not easily give up, who is unruffled by enmities, someone who will not persist in wrongdoing, who will not hesitate to pursue right once he knows it, someone whose heart knows no greed, who will not be satisfied with a minimum of explanation without seeking the maximum of understanding, who will be the most steadfast when doubt is cast, who will be the least impatient in correcting the opponent, the most patient in pursuing the truth, the most stern in meting out judgment; someone who is unaffected by flattery and not swayed by temptation and these are but few.

Ali has been regarded throughout history as one of the most influential individuals mankind has witnessed. To the Shia, he is the First Imam, true successor of God's last prophet, and the most perfect exemplar of man, second only to Muhammad. To the Sunnis, he is the brave warrior that defended Islam from his youth and the fourth of the "Rightly Guided Caliphs." To non-Muslims he is an inspiration and an example of human excellence.

Washington Irving (1783-1859), known as the "first American man of letters," described Ali as "the noblest branch of the noble race of Koreish. He possessed the three qualities most prized by Arabs: courage, eloquence, and munificence. His intrepid spirit had gained him from the prophet the appellation of The Lion of God, specimens of his eloquence remain in some verses and sayings preserved among the Arabs; and his munificence was manifested in sharing among others, every Friday, what remained in the treasury. Of his magnanimity, we have given repeated instances; his noble scorn of everything false and mean, and the absence in his conduct of everything like selfish intrigue."[31]

---

[31] Washington Irving, Lives of the Successors of Mahomet: p. 165. Published in 1850, London, UK.

Scottish historian and writer, Thomas Carlyle (1795-1881), admired Ali so much that he said, "As for this young Ali, one cannot but like him. A noble-minded creature, as he shows himself, now and always afterwards; full of affection, of fiery daring. Something chivalrous in him; brave as a lion; yet with a grace, a truth and affection worthy of Christian knighthood."[32]

Simon Ockley (1678-1720) – Professor of Arabic at the University of Cambridge – said, "One thing particularly deserving to be noticed is that his mother was delivered of him at Mecca, in the very temple itself; which never happened to any one else."[33] Gerald de Gaury (1897 - 1984), a distinguished soldier and diplomat, praised Ali saying, "He had been wise in counsel and brave in battle, true to his friends and magnanimous to his foes. He was to be for ever the paragon of Muslim nobility and chivalry."[34]

The list of notable figures who have spoken on the greatness of Ali goes on, as our mentioning here intends only to share a taste of inspiration that has been experienced by generation after generation.

Imam Ali was assassinated at the hands of the extremist Abdul Rahman ibn Muljam on the 21st of the month of Ramadan in 40 AH, January 28, 661 AD in the Mosque of Kufa. He was buried in the Holy City of Najaf, Iraq. The Shrine of Imam Ali in Najaf is one of the most revered and visited shrines of the Islamic world today.

Imam Hassan ibn Ali

(3 - 50 AH / 625 – 670 AD)

---

[32] Thomas Carlyle, On Heroes, Hero-Worship, And The Heroic In History, 1841, Lecture 2: The Hero as Prophet. Mahomet: Islam, May 8, 1840.

[33] Simon Ockley, History of the Saracens: p. 331. Published in 1894, London, UK.

[34] Geral de Guary, Rulers of Mecca: p. 49. Published in 1951, London, UK.

Hassan was the first child of Fatima bint Muhammad and Ali ibn Abi Talib. He was born in the Holy City of Medina. Hassan ibn Ali grew up in the arms of the Prophet. Narrations tell us that the Prophet would frequently sit Hassan and Hussain, Hassan's younger brother, on his lap when he sat with his companions and advised them. As the Prophet beamed in joy with his precious grandsons, he would smile and say to his companions, "Hassan and Hussain are the Princes of the Youth of Paradise…"[35]

Hassan ibn Ali grew up to be a man of character and wisdom, just like his father Ali. He was widely known for his morality, forgiveness, and kindness to even those that had deeply wronged him. He was judicious in his application of Islamic law, maintaining social justice, and empowering the people of the nation. Imam Hassan learned much from his father in striking a balance of ensuring social justice and minimizing discord and strife in the Muslim community. In striking such a balance, he sacrificed much of himself as his father and grandfather had done. Sacrifice became characteristic of the Household of Muhammad, as every member of the family would give their life to protect the principles of the faith.

After the death of his father, Imam Hassan became the Caliph of the Muslims. This however was met with heavy opposition by the stronghold of Muawiya, the son of Abu Sufyan, in Syria. Abu Sufyan was a chieftain of Mecca and one of the first arch-enemies of the Prophet. Abu Sufyan only came to the faith after surrendering to the army of Muslims that marched back to Mecca lead by their prophet. When Abu Sufyan saw the grand army of Muhammad in their return to Mecca, he turned to the Prophet's uncle Abbas and said, "It seems like your nephew's possessions and dominion have expanded greatly." Abbas gazed

---

[35] Fada'il Al-Sahaba, by Ahmad Hanbal, v2, p771, Tradition #1360.

upon the long ranks of the Prophet's soldiers and responded, "Rather, it is the Prophecy."[36]

Muawiya had campaigned against Imam Ali and his sons for years, so much so that the cursing of Ali ibn Abi Talib was institutionalized in the Friday prayer sermons across Syria. Imam Hassan realized the challenges that lied ahead. Muawiya was mobilizing his forces of sixty thousand soldiers to wage war on Imam Hassan, just as he did on his father Ali in the Battle of Siffin. The Battle of Siffin was the second civil war waged on Ali as Caliph, led by Muawiya. Edward Gibbon (1737-1794), an English historian and Member of Parliament, described that in the battle, "The Caliph Ali displayed a superior character of valor and humanity. His troops were strictly enjoined to wait the first onset of the enemy, to spare their flying brethren, and to respect the bodies of the dead, and the chastity of the female captives. The ranks of the Syrians were broken by the charge of the hero, who was mounted on a piebald horse, and wielded with irresistible force, his ponderous and two edged sword."[37]

Imam Hassan was one of his father's generals standing at the forefront of command and leadership in defending the Islamic nation against the threats of the likes of Muawiya. Hassan knew very well of Muawiya's malicious intentions and mischievous capabilities. Though he and his father were victorious at Siffin, as Muawiya's forces surrendered and raised the white flag, this time was different. Imam Hassan's troops were not as formidable as they once were under his father. Muawiya's spies had infiltrated his ranks and bribed a number of the troops to betray their Caliph. Betray they did. Imam Hassan made a judgment call. With an unreliable army, and a thirsty enemy that supposedly attached itself to the same faith, he realized it

[36] Sayyid Ali Al-Hakeem, Duroos min Al-Islam: vol. 4, p. 16.
[37] Edward Gibbon, The Rise and Fall of the Roman Empire (London, 1848) vol. 3, p. 522.

would not be wise to engage in a war that would spill the blood of thousands only to further fuel the cause of the Umayyads.

Knowing that Muawiya will only persist in his warmongering and sacrilege, Imam Hassan decided to safeguard the blood of the Muslims and the strength of Islam by stepping down from the Caliphate. In no way was this to be considered as surrendering to Muawiya or recognizing him as Caliph. The members of the Prophet's Household had their rights stripped from them before – their silence was not a sign of contentment, it was a stance of patience and protest. Imam Hassan signed a peace treaty with Muawiya containing the following specific conditions:

1. Authority will be handed to Muawiya provided that he should act according to the Book of Allah, the Sunna (Tradition) of the Prophet,[38] and the behavior of the righteous Caliphs.[39]

2. Authority should be for Imam Hassan after Muawiya.[40] If Imam Hassan predeceases Muawiya, then authority should go to Imam Hussain.[41] Muawiya had no right to entrust authority to anyone.[42]

3. Muawiya must abandon the cursing of the Commander of the Faithful (Imam Ali) and the practice of supplicating against him in prayers.[43] Muawiya should not

---

[38] Al-Hadid, Ibn Abu. Sharh Nahj Al-Balagha, vol. 4. p. 6.

[39] Al-Nasaih Al-Kafiya. p. 156, and Bihar Al-Anwar, vol. 10. p. 115.

[40] Tarikh Al-Khulafa. p. 194; Al-Bidaya wa alNahaya, vol. 8. p. 41; Al-Asqalani, Ahmad Shahab Al-Din. Al-Isaba fi Tamiiz Al-Sahaba, vol. 2. pp. 12, 13; Al-Dinawari, Ibn Qutayba. Al-Imama wa Al-Siyasa. p. 150; and Wajdi, Farid. Dairat Al-Marif Al-Islamiya, vol. 3. p. 443.

[41] Umdat Al-Talib. p. 52.

[42] Sharh Nahj Al-Balagha, vol. 4. p. 8; Bihar Al-Anwar, vol. 10. p. 115; and Al-Fusw al Muhimma.

[43] Al-Amili, Muhsin Al-Amin. A'yan Al-Shia, vol. 4. p. 43.

bring mentioning or utter the name Ali unless it is in a good manner.[44]

4. Muawiya is to be excluded from what lies in the treasury of Kufa – an amount of five million dirhams. Muawiya must send the Imam one million dirhams a year. He is to give preference to the descendants of Banu Hashim (the Prophet's tribe) in what is given in gifts over the descendants of Banu Abd Shams (the Umayyads). Furthermore, he is to divide one million dirhams among the sons of those who were killed with the Commander of the Faithful at the Battle of the Camel and the Battle of Siffin. This should be spent from the taxes of Dar Abjard.[45]

5. The people should be safe wherever they are on God's Earth. Muawiya must ensure security and safety for all people of all races. The companions of Imam Ali should be ensured security wherever they are. Muawiya should not seek calamity or harm secretly or openly for Imam Hassan, nor for Imam Hussein, nor for any of the Prophet's AhlulBayt (Household).[46]

Muawiya did not honor a single condition of the peace treaty. His governance was the farthest from the principles of Islam and its Prophet. Not only did he neglect to forbid the cursing of Ali, he gave special orders to government instituted preachers and orators to curse Ali in every sermon they delivered. The Shia and companions of Imam Ali were persecuted, discriminated against, marginalized and executed. Muawiya even appointed his son Yazid, a blasphemous drunkard, as the next

---

[44] Al-Isfahani, Abu Al-Faraj. Maqatil Al-Talibiyyin. p. 26, and al Hadid, Ibn Abu. Sharh Nahj Al-Balagha, vol. 4. p. 15.

[45] Al-Dinawari, Ibn Qutayba. Al-Imama wa Al-Siyasa. p. 200; Tarikh, vol. 6. p. 92; Ilal Al-Sharaiya. p. 81; and Al-Bidaya wa Al-Nihaya, vol. 8. p. 14.

[46] Al-Kamil fi Al-Tarikh, vol. 3. p. 166; Al-Isfahani, Abu Al-Faraj. Maqatil Al-Talibiyyin. p. 26; al Hadid, Ibn Abu. Sharh Nahj Al-Balagha, vol. 4. p. 15; and Bihar Al-Anwar, vol. 10. p. 115.

Caliph. There was no glory in the reign of Muawiya, only filth and disgrace that tainted the history of Muslims.

Imam Hassan gave us undying guidance not only through his sacrifice but also through the words of wisdom he left behind. He advised his followers to pay specific attention to a set of morals. He said, "There are ten morals: honesty of the tongue, sincerity of valor, giving to the needy, good manners, reward through actions, blood relations, protecting the neighbor, justice for its rightful owner, hospitality and most importantly, modesty."[47]

Imam Hassan was martyred by poison at the behest of the Umayyad ruler Muawiya ibn Abi Sufyan in 50 AH / 670 AD. He was buried in the Holy City of Medina.

Imam Hussain ibn Ali

(4 - 61 AH / 626 – 680 AD)

The second son of Fatima and Ali, Hussain was born in the Holy City of Medina. Hussain shared the same honor and distinction that his older brother Hassan had. He was intent on correcting the course of Islamic rule and hold Muslim rulers accountable for their conduct and policies. He thereby refuted the false idea that a ruler has immunity from criticism and accountability to the people. The Umayyads indoctrinated people to believe that the ruler must be obeyed blindly and never to be questioned regardless of the degree of his injustice and infringement. Muawiya and the rest of the Umayyad dynasty put much effort to infiltrate Islamic culture and education with these false principles of rule, which has influenced Muslim culture of governance to this day. Imam Hussain countered those sentiments when he stood up to the oppressor Yazid ibn

---

[47] Tareekh al Ya'koubi: 2/226.

Muawiya despite the lack of military parity between the two parties.

Before embarking on his journey of undying sacrifice, Imam Hussain gave instructions to his brother Muhammad ibn Al-Hanafiyya saying, "I do not leave with ill intentions or for naught and nor as a corruptor or an oppressor. Rather I leave to ask for reform in my grandfather's nation. I want to enjoin the good and prohibit evil. My path is that of my grandfather and my father Ali ibn Abi Talib. He who accepts me accepts righteousness; God is more worthy of righteousness. He who opposes me, I will endure until God judges between me and the people by that which is right and He is the best of judges..."[48]

On the 10th of Muharram[49] in the year 61 AH (10/10/680 AD), Yazid's army of over thirty thousand surrounded the caravan of Imam Hussain in the land of Karbala, Iraq. Hussain was accompanied by his family, women and children, and seventy-two of his loyal companions. He was making his way to Kufa, Iraq to answer the call of those oppressed by Umayyad rule. They had sent him thousands of letters to come to their aid and lead them as his brother and father once did. Before reaching Kufa, Imam Hussain was stopped in Karbala by Yazid's army led by Omar ibn Saad. Unwilling to surrender and having no crime to which to confess, Hussain and his companions stood firm in the face of the odds against them. Along with his sons, brothers, nephews and seventy-two loyal companions, Hussain was brutally killed and martyred. He was beheaded, his body trampled by horses, and his head placed on a spear.[50] This was done to every martyr whodefended Hussain

---

[48] Al-Kafee: 5/59-60 and Al-Foutouh: 5/33.

[49] The first month of the Islamic calendar.

[50] We find similar behavior is being practiced by the current Salafist terrorist movements following the path of their predecessors.

on what became known as the Day of Ashura. Women, children, and the elderly were not spared.

Those who survived were taken as prisoners. Beaten, whipped, and humiliated, they were paraded through the streets of Kufa and Damascus, with the bloody heads of their loved ones towering over them on spears. Yazid personally instructed his commanders to order the soldiers to parade the captives in such a manner. He wanted to demoralize Hussain's family. He wanted to show them his wrath. When the captive women and children finally arrived in Yazid's court in Damascus, he boasted his "victory" over the Prophet's grandson. He gloated in poetic verses wishing that his forefathers were present to witness such a proud day where Banu Umayya triumphed over Banu Hashim.

Little did Yazid know that his "victory" awakened the conscience of a nation; A nation that was dead in its moral conscience for over twenty years under Umayyad rule. Imam Hussain's stance against Yazid was more than a battle, a massacre, or an unjust crime – it was a revolution that transcended time. Imam Hussain became a symbol of freedom and justice for Muslims and even non-Muslims everywhere. He inspired generation after generation through his unwavering insistence on the true application of social justice. His timeless revolution etched in Islamic thought the doctrine of governance that there is no immunity for unjust rulers under any circumstance, time or place. Hussain and his companions displayed every principle of Islam – justice, mercy, equality, sacrifice, and brotherhood – in their stance of bravery and courage against the tyrant Yazid.

All around the world, millions of Shia Muslims commemorate the martyrdom of the champions of Karbala on the 10th of Muharram. They express the depth of their sorrow at their killing and orators take to the podiums to remind the people of the religious and humanitarian values for which Imam Hussain and those who followed him sacrificed their lives. They urge their listeners to hold on to Imam Hussain's path of righteousness and justice. Shia scholars, lecturers and eulogizers emphasize that Imam Hussain's revolution was purposed in rejecting injustice, deviation, and the reverence of dictators. Imam Hussain stood for freedom, people's inalienable rights to life and liberty, and the accountability of those who govern over us.

Imam Hussain's revolution continues to inspire millions of people, Muslim and non-Muslim alike. Numerous international personalities have praised Imam Hussain's eternal stand of justice and sacrifice. From philosophers and scholars to politicians and diplomats, Hussain serves as an inspiration for every freedom-loving heart.

British philosopher Bertrand Russell[51] said, "Humanity should be proud of Hussain who exploded the largest volcano and uprooted the tyrannical rulers who oppressed their people. The fire of this volcano threw them into the swamp of immorality, a place they deserve."[52]

Johann Wolfgang von Goethe,[53] a renowned German literary figure, remarked that, "The tragedy of Hussain is a tragedy for the entire human conscience. Hussain was the body of the hu-

---

[51] English philosopher, athlete and author (1872-1970). He was awarded a Nobel Prize in 1950. He wrote over one hundred books and many articles about philosophy, psychology, sociology, politics, religion, morality, and sex. His work includes principles of mathematics, the history of Western philosophy and problems in philosophy.

[52] As quoted from brief sayings about Imam Hussain; prepared by Muhammad Hameed Al-Sawaf, Shabakat Al-Naba' Al-Ma'loumatiyah; 10th of Muharam 1430 AH / 7th of January 2009 AD.

[53] Born in Frankfurt in 1749 and died in Weimar in 1832 AD. He was considered one of the most famous and important literary figures in the history of German and world literature. He wrote poetry, plays, and novels. Aside from literature, he was interested in the physical sciences. He managed a theater and held political positions in Weimar.

man conscience because of his defense of human values and good example."[54]

Mahatma Gandhi, the liberator of India, has famously said, "I learned from Hussain how to achieve victory while being oppressed."[55]

Edward Gibbon also commented on the tragedy of Karbala saying, "In a distant age and climate, the tragic scene of the death of Hosein will awaken the sympathy of the coldest reader."[56]

Scottish orientalist Sir William Muir made a stunning observation that, "The tragedy of Karbala decided not only the fate of the Caliphate, but also of Mohammadan kingdoms long after the Caliphate had waned and disappeared."[57]

A hundred years later, Eastern European orientalist Ignaz Goldziher commented specifically on the mourning of the Tragedy of Karbala. He said, "...Weeping and lamentation over the evils and persecutions suffered by the 'Alid[58] family, and mourning for its martyrs: these are things from which loyal supporters of the cause cannot cease. 'More touching than the tears of the Shi'is' has even become an Arabic proverb."[59]

Perhaps Edward G. Brown, a Professor at the University of Cambridge in the early 20th century, sums it up most eloquently when he reflects on the events that took place on the plains

---

[54] See Imam Hussain Mashrou' Hadhari Lel-Taghyeer by Hilal Fakhr Al-Deen, Ashoura, 1430, Shabakat Al-Naba' Al-Ma'loumatiyah.

[55] Koussat Tajareebee ma' Al-Hakeeka. See also, Darsee Kah Hussain Beh Insanha Amoukht: p. 441.

[56] Edward Gibbon, The Decline and Fall of the Roman Empire: vol. 5, p. 391-392. Published in 1911, London, UK.

[57] Sir William Muir, Annals of the Early Caliphate: p. 441-442. Published in 1883, London, UK.

[58] Alid is a term used to refer to those who were from the lineage or bloodline of Imam Ali ibn Abi Talib.

[59] Ignaz Goldziher, Introduction to Islamic Theology and Law: p. 179. Princeton, 1981.

of Karbala. He writes, "...a reminder of that blood-stained field of Karbala, where the grandson of the Apostle of God fell, at length, tortured by thirst, and surrounded by the bodies of his murdered kinsmen, has been at anytime since then, sufficient to evoke, even in the most lukewarm and the heedless, the deepest emotion, the most frantic grief, and an exaltation of spirit before which pain, danger, and death shrink to unconsidered trifles."[60]

Imam Ali Zayn Al-Abideen

(38 - 99 AH / 658 – 717 AD)

Imam Ali Zayn Al-Abideen was born in the Holy City of Medina – the son of Imam Hussain ibn Ali. Zayn Al-Abideen was present during the Tragedy of Karbala; however, due to illness his father had prohibited him from participating in battle. There was divine wisdom in Zayn Al-Abideen's illness, as his father explained to him – he would be the next Imam of the Shia after Hussain's martyrdom. Zayn Al-Abideen was taken as a prisoner, along with the surviving women and children, at the close of the battle. They were dragged as captives from Karbala to Damascus – the Umayyad capitol.

The tribulation that Zayn Al-Abideen went through was unmatched. He witnessed the massacre of his father, brothers, uncles and friends, unable to come to their aid. He saw the women and children of his family abused at the hands of tyrant militants. He was taken captive, beaten with rods and whips. They laughed as they carried the head of his father on a spear. They cursed his grandfather Ali. They wanted to break him. Still, he remained patient and persevered through it all. He was resilient. He had to be. He was the protector of the faith after

---

[60] Edward G. Brown, A Literary History of Persia: p. 227. Published in 1919, London, UK.

his father, and even though so many stood against him, he was there to reawaken their souls and bring them back to the religion for which his father died.

Zayn Al-Abideen spent his days teaching and writing. His teaching touched on the social and political dimensions of the nation's current affairs. He cared for the people, ill and poor, displaying the grace and kindness of his grandfather Ali ibn Abi Talib. He also placed a great emphasis on spiritual awakening and development. He led by practice – known for the most pristine prayers and most eloquent heart wrenching supplications. Many of his supplications are compiled in a book known as "Al-Saheefah Al-Sajadeeyah" – the Psalms of Islam.

Despite the oppression he faced with his family, Zayn Al-Abideen continued to look at the greater good as his forefathers always had. As the Imam, he was a mercy to all – even those who had oppressed him. Thus, he would receive the followers of the Umayyad rulers with grace and open arms, answering their questions and providing them with guidance and wisdom. In addition to the Psalms of Islam, Zayn Al-Abideen wrote "Risalat Al-Huquq" – the Treatise on Rights. This treatise outlined fifty different rights that exist between people, as between themselves, and their relationship with God. He particularly explained that there are rights that individuals owe to themselves and to each of their body parts. The treatise begins with the rights prescribed to God and ends with the rights between family members and of members of society towards each other.

On the right of the mother, Imam Zayn Al-Abideen said the following: "The right of your mother is that you know that she carried you where no one carries anyone, she gave to you of the fruit of her heart that which no one gives to anyone, and she protected you with all her organs. She did not care if she went hungry as long as you ate, if she was thirsty as long as you drank, if she was unclothed as long as you were clothed, if she was in the sun as long as you were in the shade. She gave up sleep for your sake, she protected you from heat and cold, all in order that you might belong to her... You will not be able to show her gratitude, without God's help...".[61]

Observing the aftermath of Imam Hussain's gruesome murder, the tyrants that targeted the members of the Prophet's household refrained from using such risky tactics in getting rid of the Imams. Thus, starting with Imam Zayn Al-Abideen and for each of the Imams after him, death by poison was employed instead. Zayn Al-Abideen was poisoned in 717 AD and buried in the Baqee' cemetery in Medina.

Imam Muhammad Al-Baqir

(57 - 114 AH / 677 – 732 AD)

Imam Muhammad Al-Baqir – the son of Imam Zayn Al-Abideen – was born in the Holy City of Medina and was known for his vast amount of knowledge and as such was titled Al-Baqir, which means *he who erupts knowledge and deepens it*. Abdullah ibn Ata Al-Makki described the Imam when he said, "I have not seen scholars visiting with someone younger than themselves except Abu Jaafar Muhammad ibn Ali ibn Hussain."[62]

Imam Al-Baqir laid the foregrounds of what became known as the Jaafari School of Thought – named after his son Imam Jaafar Al-Sadiq who continued the work of his father. This school of thought was fueled by the authentic teachings of the Prophet and Imam Ali. It became a cultivation center for Shia

---

[61] Imam Ali Zayn Al-Abideen, Treatise on Rights. Right #22.
[62] Al-Irshad: p. 263.

theology, philosophy and culture, which has expanded and endured the test of time. Its most prominent characteristics were its salient understanding of the inherent teachings of the Quran and the Prophet, and its independence from the dictatorships that plagued Muslim nation. The Jaafari School was particularly unique in being free of associating with or producing any false or extremist texts on the principles of religion.

Imam Al-Baqir was described as embodying the most excellent virtues of humanity, respected for his knowledge and character amongst friends and foes. He advised his followers to be kind to others and to speak to them in a way that they would like others to speak to them. He said, "Tell people the best of what you would desire to be said to you, for God loathes the wicked who curses and backbites the believers."[63]

The Imam was poisoned and died in 732 AD. He was buried in the Bakee' cemetery in Medina.

Imam Jaafar Al-Sadiq

(80 - 148 AH / 699 – 765 AD)

Imam Jaafar Al-Sadiq was born in Medina – the son of Imam Muhammad Al-Baqir. He lived through the decline of the Umayyads and the rise of Abbasids, witnessing their political and military conflicts. As the Umayyads and Abbasids were busy with their struggle for the seat of the Caliphate, Imam Al-Sadiq took advantage of the opportunity to further develop and expand the school of thought that his father established. The school of thought was attributed to Imam Jaafar and became known as the Jaafari School of Thought. He drew up a general strategy to deepen and spread his school of thought by growing a large number of scholars in various scientific disci-

---

[63] A'yan Al-Shia: 1/656.

plines. The students and scholars who studied and taught under Imam Al-Sadiq delved into philosophy, theology, jurisprudence, Quranic exegesis, and even mathematics, physics, physiology, chemistry and other empirical sciences. An example of the products of the Jaafari School was the world-renowned Jaber ibn Hayan Al-Kufi. Jaber was a prominent Muslim polymath: chemist and alchemist, astronomer, geographer, engineer, philosopher, physicist, pharmacist and physician – a humble student of Imam Jaafar Al-Sadiq.

Imam Al-Sadiq's motivation was fueled by his father's last words. Our narrations say that shortly before Imam Al-Baqir's death, he looked at his son Jaafar and said, "I ask you to do well by my companions..." To that the loyal son replied to his father earnestly, "By God, I will support them and ensure that every man amongst them will not seek anyone else's help in whatever land he may be in."[64]

Imam Al-Sadiq not only expanded the school of thought of Ahlulbayt, he provided inspiration to his followers with the most simple of words. He reminded the Muslims of what it meant to be a true believer in God. He told them and showed them by his immaculate character and conduct. He told his followers to pay attention to their souls and be mindful of their traits. He said that there are, "Six characteristics that are not present in a believer: poverty, bad temper, envy, importunity, lying, and oppression."[65]

Imam Jaafar Al-Sadiq was poisoned and died in the year 765 AD. He was buried in the Bakee' cemetery in Medina, next to his father and grandfather.

---

[64] I'lam Al-Wara bee A'lam Al-Houda: 1/517.
[65] Touhaf Al-Okoul: 376.

Imam Moussa Al-Kadhim

(128 - 183 AH / 746 – 799 AD)

Imam Moussa Al-Kadhim was the son of Imam Jaafar Al-Sadiq. He was born in the City of Medina. Our narrations tell us that his mother was a pious woman from Andalusia – present day Spain.

From a young age, Al-Kadhim displayed maturity, knowledge and wisdom. He would accompany his father and be of assistance to him as early as the age of five, answering people's questions on matters of theology, philosophy, and jurisprudence. As he grew older and took the responsibility of Imamah after his father died, he also addressed the social problems that were festering with the growth of the Abbasids. He focused on addressing the social corruption that had spread as a result of the affluence and financial corruption that was rampant in the governing body at the time. As such, he faced the iron fist of the two Abbasid rulers, Moussa Al-Hadi and Harun Al-Rashid. The Abbasids were no less than the Umayyads in their tyranny; they just hid it better.

One day, as Imam Al-Kadhim was walking in a neighborhood he heard music and laughter coming out of one particular home. The man who lived there was an affluent man by the name of Bishr. Bishr was keen to gatherings of entertainment, drinking, music and dancing. As he got closer to the house, the Imam noticed one of the house servants come out of the house carrying a large basket. The basket was full of the leftovers of dark red grapes that had been apparently squeezed dry to make wine. The house servant pursued to toss the squished grapes in a pile of rubbish. As she was busy emptying her basket, the Imam approached her. He asked, "Who does this house belong to?" Still busy emptying her basket she replied, "It is for my master, Bishr."

"Is your master a free man or a slave?" asked the Imam. Boggled by his question, she brings her basket down and looks up puzzled. "I just said that my *master* Bishr owns this house, and you reply by asking if he is a free man or a slave? Of course he is a free man! Could anyone other than the free have a house and servants?"

"You're right. If he was a slave he would have obeyed his Master [God]," the Imam replied to her and walked away. The house servant went back into the house and told Bishr of the conversation she just had. With a peculiar combination of interest and worry, Bishr asked her to describe the man. "What did he say exactly?" Bishr asked.

"He said, 'You're right. If he was a slave he would have obeyed his Master.' What does that mean?" she replied. Bishr immediately jumped up from his lavish gathering and ran out of the house barefoot desperately searching for the man who spoke with his maid . He spotted the Imam walking down the street, ran toward him and kneeled before him. Bishr kissed the hands of Al-Kadhim and asked him for forgiveness, for he had understood the words of Al-Kadhim. The Imam granted him forgiveness and prayed for him. Bishr changed his ways and became known as a man of humility and honor.[66]

He was known for his empathy, forbearance and patience. The Imam had particularly endured through numerous straining circumstances and years of imprisonment under Abbasid rule. He became known as Al-Kadhim for his epoch-making restraint, control, and fortitude in spite of such challenges.

---

[66] Sayyid Ali Al-Hakeem, Duroos min Al-Islam: vol. 2, p. 55.

Harun Al-Rashid ordered to have Imam Al-Kadhim brought to Baghdad – the new capital of the Caliphate – so he could keep him under close watch. For several years he was arrested on baseless charges and imprisoned out of fear of his growing influence over the people. His Shia and admirers continued to be harassed and persecuted.

Like his fathers, Imam Al-Kadhim was killed by poison. He died in 799 AD. Situated in the suburb of Baghdad known as Al-Kadhimiya, his shrine is a frequently visited destination for Shia Muslim pilgrims.

Imam Ali Al-Rida

(148 - 203 AH / 765 – 818 AD)

Imam Ali Al-Rida was born in Medina – the son of Imam Moussa Al-Kadhim. Al-Rida was raised in a household that produced him to be an exemplar of virtue and wisdom, to friends and foes alike. He was instrumental in opposing the ramifications that came out of the bloody conflict for power between the two Abbasids brothers, Al-Amin and Al-Ma'moun; a conflict that killed tens of thousands and resulted in much destruction and devastation.

The struggle of power between the Abbasid brothers also resulted in the growth of atheism along with a few other misguided ideologies. The Imam and his students sparred with these groups through dialogue and scientific debate. Much of the great debates that took place in this era were attributed to Imam Al-Rida, bringing great honor to Islam. He was able to answer the inquisitions of foreigners in their own languages and address the flaws in their own ideologies and beliefs. His position of knowledge and wisdom was undeniable, and he had an aura about him that attracted young and old. Al-Ma'moun overcame his brother Al-Amin and became Caliph. In an effort to gain legitimacy amongst the growing Shia population, he summoned Imam Al-Rida to Khorasan in modern day Iran. In his court, sitting on the throne of the Caliphate Al-Ma'moun told Al-Rida that he wanted to give up the position and hand it over to him. Imam Al-Rida eloquently responded, "If this caliphate belongs to you, then it is not befitting for you to take off the garment in which God has clothed you. If the caliphate does not belong to you, then it is not permissible for you to give me that which you do not own."

Al-Ma'moun tried what he could to involve the Imam in the Abbasid government to ensure the stability of his rule and the calm of the Shia. He attempted to appoint the Imam as his ruling heir, Al-Rida refused. As the years passed, the influence of Imam Al-Rida grew and the population of Shia increased. Al-Ma'moun followed the tradition of the caliphs before him and had the Imam poisoned in the city of Tus as he was coming back from Khorasan to Baghdad. Imam Al-Rida was buried there and his resting place is preserved today in his shrine in the city of Mashhad in northeast Iran.

Despite the political pressure that he endured, Al-Rida continued to inspire the followers of Islam. He emphasized the importance of intellect and knowledge telling his followers, "The friend of every man is his mind. A man's enemy is his own ignorance."[67]

He also described to his followers what it meant to be a true believer. He said, "If a believer became angry, his anger will not stray him away from what is right. And if he was satisfied, his satisfaction will not take him to falsehood. And if he had power, he will not assume more than he deserves."

---

[67] A'yan Al-Shia: 2/26.

Imam Muhammad Al-Jawad

(195 - 220 AH / 811 – 835 AD)

Son of Imam Ali Al-Rida, Imam Muhammad Al-Jawad was born in the Abbasid capital of Baghdad. Imam Al-Jawad was only about seven years old when his father died. He assumed the responsibility of divine leadership at such a young age and nonetheless had the most striking display of knowledge and wisdom.

One day, Al-Ma'moun went hunting accompanied by his entourage. On their way, they passed through a road where a group of boys were playing. Among the boys was Imam Al-Jawad. When the caliph's horsemen approached, the boys scattered, but Al-Jawad remained in his spot. In the middle of the road, the young Imam looked at Al-Ma'moun as he approached. The caliph stopped his carriage and asked, "Boy, what kept you from running away with the others?"

"The road was not so narrow that I should fear there would not be enough room for you to pass. Nor am I guilty of any crime that I should feel scared and choose to run. I considered that you were the sort of man who would not injure one who had done no wrong," answered the young Imam. Al-Ma'moun was both delighted and intrigued by Al-Jawad's response.

Upon returning from his hunting trip, Al-Ma'moun saw the young Imam again. During the trip, one of Al-Ma'moun's falcons brought him a small fish. He took that fish and concealed it in his fist and asked Al-Jawad, "Can you tell me what I have in my hand?"

"Our Creator created all living things on land and in the sea. Of His creation he placed small fish in the sea. Those fish are hunted by the falcons of kings and caliphs that take such fish in their fists and try the sons of Muhammad with it,"[68] was the eloquent reply of the young Imam.

It was soon after this that Al-Ma'moun called for a large gathering of scholars to test the young Imam's knowledge. Within minutes all those in attendance were astonished by the eloquence, analysis, and knowledge of the Imam. The Abbasid ruler Al-Ma'moun was so impressed that he pledged that he would marry his own daughter to the Imam.

Al-Ma'moun's brother on the other hand, Al-Mu'tassim Al-Abbassi, who ruled after Al-Ma'moun, was not fond of the growing popularity of the young Imam. Thus, soon after he took the seat of the caliphate he ordered Al-Jawad poisoned. He was only 25 years old when he died. He was buried next to his grandfather Imam Al-Kadhim in Al-Kadhimia today.

At his young age, he led his followers by example. He was known as Al-Jawad for being so generous – never denying a soul who asked for help and giving to those who did not expect it. Imam Al-Jawad advised his followers to be thankful for their blessings. He said, "The blessing that is not thanked becomes a sin that is not forgiven."[69] He also said, "He who preaches to his brother in private, respects him and he who preaches to his brother in public, insults him."[70]

Imam Ali Al-Hadi

(212 - 254 AH / 827 – 868 AD)

Like his father, Imam Ali Al-Hadi also assumed the responsibility leading the followers of Ahlulbayt at a very young age. He was eight years old when Imam Al-Jawad was killed. Al-

---

[68] Sharif Al-Qarashi, The Life of Imam Muhammad Al-Jawad: p. 206.
[69] Sharif Al-Qarashi, The Life of Imam Muhammad Al-Jawad: p. 116.
[70] The Encyclopedia of Imam Al-Jawad: 2/353.

Hadi lived in a time that was especially characteristic of power struggles within the Abbasid dynasty. Four caliphs would rise and be deposed one after the other during the life of Imam Al-Hadi. Though turmoil was evident amongst them, they all shared spite for the Imam and his forefathers.

Known for his knowledge and ethics, the Imam aimed to safeguard the people from the ramifications of these internal conflicts that led to social and intellectual turbulence in the Muslim community. He focused on developing the human infrastructure of the community through education, intellectual debates, caring for the poor, and serving as an example and role model.

The stories of the Imams lives were very similar in this aspect. They served the people, helped them grow, inspired them, and made them better. Their popularity and influence would grow, despite their humbleness and humility – something that angered those who sat at the throne of the caliphate. Like his forefathers, Al-Hadi was summoned by the Abbasid ruler to leave Medina. Al-Mutawakil was the ruler at the time, infamous for his cruelty, envy and hatred for the family of the Prophet. This time the Imam was brought to the city of Samarra, located about 120 km from Baghdad.

Like all the Imams before him from the lineage of Imam Hussain, Al-Hadi was oppressed, placed under house arrest, and eventually poisoned. He was buried in that same city, which is now home to the Al-Askari shrine in which he and his son Imam Hassan Al-Askari are buried. This shrine was the target of extremist Salafi terrorists both in 2006 and 2007. Their attack on the shrine not only destroyed its monumental golden dome but also devastated the hearts of Muslims all around the world. Nonetheless, the Shia were resilient and persevered calling for unity with their Muslim brothers and sisters in Iraq. The security situation was stabilized and the threats of terrorism were controlled. The shrine was rebuilt to stand tall in its glory and the visitors of the shrine returned to pay tribute to their Imams.

Imam Al-Hadi once said, "Beware of he who is reckless with his own self."[71] It is as if the Imam had foreshadowed the recklessness of those who would come and blow themselves up in the name of religion. These people are nothing more than criminals and terrorists. If they had an ounce of reason and faith in their hearts they would realize that every shrine they attack is a house of God, where He is glorified, praised, and worshipped. Instead, they manifest the ones about whom our Imam warned us– people who are "reckless with their own selves," killing innocent women and children. Recklessness goes hand in hand with extremism, and both are not tolerated in our faith.

Imam Hassan Al-Askari

(232 - 260 AH / 847 – 874 AD)

The Father of the Savior, Imam Hassan Al-Askari was born in the City of Medina. He was the son of Imam Ali Al-Hadi and became the father of the last of the twelve Imams – Imam Muhammad Al-Mahdi – the Awaited Savior.

Imam Al-Askari was widely recognized for his knowledge and piety. The Imam and the people of the nation lived through especially difficult circumstances because the Abbasids neglected to address the socio-economic problems that plagued their community. The Abbasid caliph and those who enjoyed the privilege of Abbasid affiliation were preoccupied with exces-

---

[71] A'yan Al-Shia: 2/36.

sively lavish lifestyles and trivial activities that created an even deeper gap between the ruling class and the people.

Imam Al-Askari drew up a plan to counter the negative ramifications of the Abbasid corruption. He sent a number of his representatives and students to different areas of the empire in an effort to help people. His students became educators and servant-leaders in each of those respective communities. The Imam's popularity subsequently grew and his unsought social status became even more prestigious in the eyes of the people. The ruling establishment became threatened by the Imam's growing presence just as it was threatened by his forefathers. By order of the Abbasid caliph, Al-Mu'tamid, Imam Al-Askari was poisoned and killed at the age of 28.

The Imam was buried in Samarra next to his father Imam Ali Al-Hadi.

Though his narrations are few in number in comparison to his forefathers, the Imam left his followers gems of wisdom that should not be neglected. "Worship is not the abundance of fasting and praying, but worship is the abundance of pondering; it is in the continuous thinking of God,"[72] the Imam said to his companions. He also advised his followers regarding faith and brotherhood. He said, "There are two qualities that are better than every other; faith in God and serving your brothers."[73]

Preaching patience and forbearance, the Imam warned his followers against the consequences of anger. He told them, "Anger is the key to all evil…"[74]

---

[72] Sharif Al-Qarashi, The Life of Imam Muhammad Al-Jawad: p. 206.
[73] Ibid.
[74] Behar Al-Anwar: 7/287.

Imam Muhammad Al-Mahdi

(Born in 255 AH / 869 AD)

Imam Muhammad Al-Mahdi was born in Samarra in 255 AH / 869 AD. Like Moses, Imam Al-Mahdi's birth was concealed due to the repressive circumstances at the time. The Abbasids were monitoring the house of Al-Askari for years, anticipating that the twelfth Imam of the Prophet's lineage would be the son of Imam Al-Askari (the eleventh Imam). But by God's grace, his birth was kept hidden from the people.

Ibn Hajar said, "He was 5 years old at the time of his father's death, however in those five years God gave him wisdom."[75]

The repressive Abbasid authorities attacked Imam Hassan Al-Askari's house upon his death in search of his son. God protected the young Imam Al-Mahdi in the same way He protected Prophet Jesus, son of Mary, when his life was threatened. The Imam was hidden from the authorities and they could find no trace of him.

Numerous narrations from the Holy Prophet and his family discuss the reemergence of Imam Al-Mahdi. Our narrations say that he will only reappear under the proper conditions. It is narrated that the Holy Prophet said, "If there were only one day left on Earth, God will prolong that day until a man of my progeny emerges to fill the Earth with justice and equality as it was once filled with injustice and oppression."[76]

Shia religious texts confirm that the emergence of Imam Al-Mahdi will coincide with the emergence of Jesus. Their roles and movements of worldwide reform will harmoniously complement one another.

---

[75] Al-Sawaek Al-Mohreekah: 208.
[76] Masnad Ahmad: 1/99 and Sounan Abi Daoud: 2/232.

At the beginning of the occultation, the Imam assigned four successive deputies that served as his direct representatives to the people. His special deputies were the following companions:

1. Uthman ibn Saeed Al-Amri (Died in 280 AH / 898 AD)
2. Muhammad ibn Uthman Al-Amri (Died in 305 AH / 917 AD)
3. Hussain ibn Rauh Al-Nawbakhti (Died in 320 AH / 932 AD)
4. Ali ibn Muhammad Al-Samari (Died in 329 AH / 941 AD)

All of the deputies lived and died in Baghdad, as it was the main center for Shia at the time.

The period of "The Four Deputies" lasted about seventy years. When the last of the deputies died, the door of direct representation to the Imam was closed and thus the major occultation began. Since then, the Shia looked towards their scholars and jurists for religious guidance.

Fifth: The Promised Judgment Day

God's justice dictates that we are accountable for our actions and how we lived our lives in this world. Thus, similar to all Muslims and followers of the Abrahamic faiths, the Shia believe that we will be resurrected to be judged for our deeds on the Final Day – the Day of Judgment. The Quran stressed this truth in response to those denying life after death saying, "And he strikes out a likeness for Us and forgets his own creation. Says he: Who will give life to the bones when they are rotten? Say: He will give life to them Who brought them into existence at first, and He is cognizant of all creation." (Quran, 36: 78-79)

These are the five foundational pillars of faith among the Shia.

Places, Events & Religious Practices

Mosques

Shia, like the rest of Muslims, look at mosques as a place of worship belonging to God Almighty. As such, Muslims often refer to a mosque as the House of God. Just as Christians and Jews hold their churches and synagogues as holy symbols of their faiths, Muslims also hold their mosques as a sanctified symbol of the Muslim faith. The mosque is the center and heart of the Muslim community. It brings Muslims together, rich and poor, young and old. It is a place to contemplate our purpose, as individuals and as a collective. It reminds us that no matter where we are in life, we are bound to return to Him. Gazing upon its mere presence teaches us that the glory of God will always be; it is up to us to stay the course and take part in it or be lost in the drifts of heedlessness. The mosque is home.

The mosque is unique and has its special status, privileges and provisions. It is the preferred and most recommended place for prayer and worship. Our narrations heavily emphasize prayer in the mosque whenever possible. It is recommended that spiritual, cultural and social activities serving individuals and the community be held in mosques.

The mosque has its own sanctity that must be observed. It is forbidden to render a mosque impure or attack it in any way. The house of God is to be respected and honored. Its surroundings are meant to be safe in Islam, for the mosque is a sanctuary and a place of refuge. None are to be harmed in the house of God.

Some mosques have an especially unique station in Islam due to their historical and religious significance. The most significant among them are the following:

1. The Kaaba and the surrounding mosque, the Grand Mosque in the Holy City of Mecca. All Muslims, Shia and non-Shia alike, hold great reverence for this mosque. The Quran talks about the Kaaba, "Most surely the first house appointed for men is the one at Bekka[77], blessed and a guidance for the nations." (Quran, 3:96). The Quran also points out that Prophet Abraham is the one who built the Kaaba and his son Ismail helped him, "And when Ibrahim and Ismail raised the foundations of the House: Our Lord! accept from us; surely Thou art the Hearing, the Knowing." (Quran, 2:127). Among the provisions of the Grand Mosque is that its sanctity is to the degree that even a convicted

---

[77] Bekka is a reference to Mecca from the Quran.

person cannot be arrested or have his sentence carried out in there. Rather, he is to be left until he leaves of his own will and then he can be arrested outside the Mosque.

2. The Prophet's Mosque in the Holy City of Medina. This mosque was built by Prophet Muhammad and the Muslims upon his migration from Mecca to Medina.

3. Jerusalem and Al-Aqsa Mosque in Jerusalem which served as the qibla (direction for prayer) for Muslims before the Kaaba.

4. The Mosque of Qiba in the Holy City of Medina.

5. The Mosque of the Two Qiblas in the Holy City of Medina. This was the mosque where Prophet Muhammad and the Muslims were praying when the Qibla was changed during their prayers from Jerusalem to the Kaaba and as such, it was called the Mosque of the Two Qiblas.

6. The Mosque of Al-Khayf in the south of Mina.

7. The Mosque of Kufa in the city of Kufa, Iraq. It was built in the year 17 AH. Imam Ali frequently led prayers in this mosque. It is also the mosque in which he was brutally assassinated while in the state of prayer. Going into prostration Imam Ali was struck on the head by Ibn Muljam's poison-dipped sword.

8. The Mosque of Sahla near Kufa.

Despite the repression the Shia have experienced over the centuries by dictators and oppressive regimes, they have managed to build their mosques in countries all across the world. Note that such repression existed not only in states where Shia were minorities, case in point – Iraq. The Shia have been a majority in Iraq for quite a long time. Nonetheless, under the fascist rule of the Baathist party Shia activities were scrutinized and constrained considerably. Repression and prohibition of free practice were intensified during the rule of the tyrant Saddam Hussein.

Burial Places of Prophets and Imams

These places are considered holy by Shia even if they are not subject to the rules of mosques. The most important of these are:

1. The Shrine of Prophet Muhammad in the Prophet's Mosque in the Holy City of Medina.
2. The Shrine of Imam Ali ibn Abi Talib, trustee to Prophet Muhammad and the first of the Imams from the family of the Prophet. It is located in the Holy City of Najaf in Iraq.
3. The cemetery in Baqee' Al-Gharkad in the Holy City of Medina where four Imams from the Prophet's family are buried. They are:
    i. Imam Hassan ibn Ali, the second Imam
    ii. Imam Ali Zayn Al-Abideen, the fourth Imam
    iii. Imam Muhammad Al-Baqir, the fifth Imam
    iv. Imam Jaafar Al-Sadiq, the sixth Imam
    v. In addition, some accounts say that Lady Fatima, Prophet Muhammad's daughter[78], is also buried there as are a large number of the companions and Islamic personalities.
4. The Shrine of Imam Hussain, the third Imam, in the city of Karbala in Iraq. Shia consider this shrine a symbol of resistance against injustice and tyranny, where Imam Hussain revolted against the tyrant Yazid and was consequently martyred along with his family and

---

[78] The burial place for Lady Fatima Al-Zahra is unknown, as she had willed that she be buried at night and her grave be hidden. The precise location of her grave remains unknown.

companions. Throughout the year, millions of Muslims visit the shrine especially during the Muharram season. Across from the Shrine of Imam Hussain is the Shrine of Al-Abbas – Imam Hussain's brother and the commander of his army who stood valiantly against the Umayyad troops in Karbala.

5. The Shrine of Imam Moussa Al-Kadhim (the seventh Imam) and Imam Muhammad Al-Jawad (the ninth Imam) in the city of Kadhimia, in the vicinity of the Iraqi capital, Baghdad.

6. The shrine of Imam Ali Al-Rida, the eighth Imam, in the city of Mashhad in Iran.

7. The Askari Shrine where Imam Ali Al-Hadi (the tenth Imam) and Imam Hassan Al-Askari (the eleventh Imam) are buried. The shrine is in the city of Samarra, Iraq.

8. The birthplace of Imam Muhammad Al-Mahdi (the twelfth Imam), which is the house of his grandfather, Imam Ali Al-Hadi, and his father, Imam Hassan Al-Askari in the city of Samarra.

The Hussainiya

In many Shia communities, Hussainiyas were constructed to provide a venue for religious, cultural and social events and functions. The Hussainiya has similar functionalities to the mosque, but does not enjoy the same rules and sanctity. The Hussainiya is best described as an Islamic center where programs and events are held.

Shia have called it – "Hussainiya" – in honor of Imam Hussain, as one of the primary functions of the center is to hold programs to commemorate his martyrdom on a yearly basis. Imam Hussain is central in Shia culture due to his monumental status in saving Islam and rejuvenating the nation through his sacrifice for justice and stance against tyranny.

Second: Religious Occasions

Throughout the Islamic calendar, you will find dates that have special value for Shia Muslims. Imam Ali said, "Surely, God has chosen for us followers (Shia), who assist us and are happy at our happiness and are sad in our sadness."[79] Much of the commemorations and celebrations that take place during the Islamic year are based on this very concept. What made the Prophet and his family happy became a cause for annual celebrations for the Shia; and what made the Prophet and his family sorrowful was reason for annual commemoration. In Shia belief, the words, actions, and traditions of the Prophet and his Household were an extension of God's revelation. So what made the Prophet and his family happy brought joy to the Shia; and what made the Prophet and his family mourn in turn made the Shia commemorate and mourn as well.

There are generally three types of religious occasions: joyous celebrations, sorrowful commemorations, and spiritual events.

Joyful Celebrations

Holidays

The Shia have four major holidays:

1. **Friday.** Every Friday is considered a holiday for all Muslims. This day of the week holds special weight for Muslims as a day of unity and community. The Muslim's Friday is very similar to Saturday for the Jews and

---

[79] Ghurar Al-Hikam: vol. 1, p. 235.

Sunday for the Christians, with of course some differentiation in the practices and customs. Every Friday, group prayers are held at the mosques whereby the spiritual leader of the mosque delivers a sermon and leads prayer. It is highly recommended to perform certain acts of worship and charity work, such as helping the poor and visiting the ill. Moreover, Friday is a day where it is especially encouraged to ensure a joyful atmosphere for the family. To make the people around you happy is considered to be a tradition of the Holy Prophet.

2. **Eid Al-Fitr.** As one of the most celebrated holidays across the Muslim world, Eid Al-Fitr marks the first day of the month of Shawwal and the conclusion of the month of Ramadan. After a whole month of fasting, giving, patience and spiritual rejuvenation, Muslims break their fast in celebration of completing their month-long obligation. People come together for Eid prayers at the mosque, exchange gifts, and visit each other in their homes. More importantly, Muslims continue giving as they did in the month of Ramadan in paying alms to the poor and needy.

3. **Eid Al-Adha.** This lands on the tenth day of the month of Dhul-Hijjah, the twelfth month in the lunar calendar. This is the day when pilgrims in Mecca are found in the area of Mena, on the outskirts of the city of Mecca, and are released from the restrictions imposed on them during the state of ihram – signifying the end of their hajj pilgrimage. On this day, it is recommended to provide and distribute food to the poor and less fortunate.

4. **Eid Al-Ghadeer.** This grand day of pride and honor falls on the 18th of Dhul-Hijjah. On this day, the Shia

celebrate the anniversary of the Prophet's appointment of Imam Ali as his successor, leader, and caliph of the Muslims. This grand event took place in an area between Mecca and Medina called Ghadeer Khum in modern day Saudi Arabia. And hence its name Eid *Al-Ghadeer*. The Shia also refer to this holiday as Eid Al-Wilaya.[80] At Ghadeer, the Prophet gathered the thousands of Muslims who were with him on his final pilgrimage and said, "Whoever I am his master, Ali is his master. O' God, be a guardian to those who pay allegiance to him and an enemy to those who are hostile to him.[81] Bring victory to those who support him and let down those who betray him."[82]

Celebration of Birthdates and Others

1. **The birthdate of Prophet Muhammad,** on the seventh day of the month of Rabi' Al-Awal, the third month in the Islamic lunar calendar.
2. **The birthdate of Imam Ali ibn Abi Talib,** on the thirteenth day of the month of Rajab, the seventh month of the Islamic lunar calendar.
3. **The birthdate of Lady Fatima Al-Zahra,** the daughter of Prophet Muhammad, on the twentieth day of the month of Jamade Al-Thanee, the sixth month of the Islamic lunar calendar.
4. **The birthdate of Imam Hassan ibn Ali,** on the 15th of the month of Ramadan, the ninth month of the Islamic lunar calendar.

---

[80] Al-Wilaya means allegiance in Arabic. The Shia refer to this day as Eid Al-Wilaya for its hallmark significance in their identity and creed.

[81] Masnad Ahmad 1: 84, 119, 152, 331.

[82] Al-Amali, Al-Sheikh Al-Moufeed: 58. Shareh Al-Akhbar, judge Nuaman Al-Maghrebee: 1/101.

5. **The birthdate of Imam Hussain ibn Ali,** on the third day of the month of Shaaban, the eighth month of the Islamic lunar calendar.

6. **The birthdate of Imam Muhammad Al-Mahdi,** on the fifteenth day of the month of Shaaban.

7. **The anniversary of the rise of the Prophet,** which signifies the beginning of the Prophet's mission of promulgating Islam and falls on the twenty-seventh day of the month of Rajab, the seventh month of the Islamic lunar calendar.

Sorrowful Commemorations

1. **The anniversary of the death of Prophet Muhammad,** on the 28th of the month of Safar, the second month of the Islamic lunar calendar. Many Shia visit Imam Ali's shrine on this anniversary to offer symbolic condolences to the Imam on the death of Prophet Muhammad, since it may not be possible for them to visit Prophet Muhammad's shrine in the Holy City of Medina.

2. **The anniversary of the martyrdom of Imam Ali,** on the 21st of month of Ramadan, the ninth month of the Islamic lunar calendar.

3. **The anniversary of the martyrdom of Lady Fatima Al-Zahra,** daughter of Prophet Muhammad. It is known to be on the 3rd of the month of Jamadee Al-Thanee, the sixth month of the Islamic lunar calendar.

4. **The anniversary of the martyrdom of Imam Hussain ibn Ali,** and his family and companions on the 10th of Muharram, the first month of the Islamic lunar calendar. This day is most notably known as the **Day of Ashura**. On this day, mourning processions are held and a general state of grief and mourning engulfs Shia worldwide. Shia commemorate the tragic killing of

Imam Hussain along with his family and 72 companions. They stood valiantly in their heroic confrontation to the army of the tyrant Yazid ibn Muawiya in Karbala. The surviving members of his family, and the relatives of the martyrs who died alongside him, were taken captive and tortured. Women and children were dragged cuffed in chains, from Karbala to Damascus and finally to the city of Medina – a travelling distance of over 2,000 km, which they walked by foot.

5. **The anniversary of the return of the families of Imam Hussain,** and those of his martyred companions from Damascus to the Holy City of Medina, passing through Karbala on the way. This falls on the 20th of the month of Safar, the second month of the Islamic lunar calendar and it is called **the Arbaeen** (the Fortieth).

Millions of Shia set out to Imam Hussain's shrine in Karbala on foot in empathy with the families of the Prophet's descendants as they returned from Damascus to Karbala on their way to the Holy City of Medina.

It is worthy to note that though these commemorations and celebrations are characteristic of Shia practice and are highly recommended to observe, they are not obligatory. Meaning, Shia are not obliged to participate in these occasions as they are obliged to perform their five daily prayers or fast in the month of Ramadan, for example.

Spiritual Events

1. **The Sacred Months.** These months include Muharram, Rajab, Dhul-Qi'da, Dhul-Hijjah. They are the first, seventh, eleventh, and twelfth months of the Islamic lunar calendar, respectively. During these months, the Shia, along with all Muslims for that matter, forbid

warfare except under necessary circumstances such as self-defense.

2. **The Holy Month of Ramadan.** During this holy month, all Muslims abstain from eating, drinking, and sexual activity, among other things, during daylight hours.

3. **The Night of Power.** The night that the Quran was revealed to Prophet Muhammad and it falls, based on the most trusted reports, on the 23rd night of the holy month of Ramadan. During this night, Shia worship God through supplications, prayers and reciting the Holy Quran. These practices are highly recommended but are not obligatory.

Third: Rituals

The Shia participate in virtually all the primary rituals that the rest of Muslims practice.

Rituals are of two kinds, mandatory and recommended.

The most important mandatory rituals are:

1. **Prayers.** The most notable of which are the five daily prayers: the Prayers of Dawn, Noon, Afternoon, Sundown and the Evening.

2. **Fasting.** As mentioned above, obligatory fasting takes place during the month of Ramadan.

3. **Pilgrimage.** During the month of Dhul-Hijjah, each able person is required to go and perform the pilgrimage rituals once in his/her lifetime.

There are numerous recommended rituals. These rituals include special prayers, fasting outside the month of Ramadan, pilgrimages to the shrines, and umrah (visiting Mecca and performing rituals aside from the pilgrimage time and its rituals).

In addition, there are volumes of supplications that serve as spiritual rejuvenation in one's relationship with God that are highly recommended. Many of these supplications can be found in Imam Zayn Al-Abideen's Saheefa Sajjadiya, or the compilation of Sheikh Al-Qumi's Mafateeh Al-Jinan. Moreover, celebrations and commemorations that revive the remembrance of the Prophet and his family, as mentioned above, also falls under the category of recommended rituals.

Money, Morals & Society

Financial Contributions

Like rituals, financial contributions in Islam also come in two forms: mandatory and recommended.

Mandatory Financial Contributions

Mandatory financial contributions include the following:

1. **Zakat** (alms) and it has two parts:
    a. Financial zakat: It varies between 2.5% and 5% as detailed in rules of jurisprudence. It is distributed to the poor and used for charitable projects and the like.
    b. Zakat for breaking fast (fitrah): It is paid to the poor usually on the day of Eid Al-Fitr and it is equal to the amount needed to feed one poor person – usually about $10 in the United States.

2. **Khums** (Tithing): Each individual is obliged to pay one fifth (20%) of his or her annual excess profits. Half of one's khums is to be spent on helping poor sayyids (individuals who are descendants of the Prophet). The other half is to be used to fund charitable, social and religious projects, per the specific requirements outlined in the texts of jurisprudence.

3. **Kaffara** (Expiations): These are levied on those who deliberately break their fast during the month of Ramadan or violate a vow or a covenant. It is spent on the poor.

4. **Fidyah** (Redemptions): These are levied on those who are unable to fast during the month of Ramadan whereby food is provided to the poor per the specific requirements outlined in the texts of jurisprudence.

Recommended Financial Contributions

Charity has been emphasized by all of God's prophets. To give charity at any time and for any noble cause is an honorable deed and is highly recommended. Other than giving directly to the poor through charity, Shia Muslims also donate to their mosques and Islamic centers in support of religious, educational, social, and civic functions.

Some communities have established endowments and grants to fund projects deemed necessary for the growth and development of the members of their community. It is worthy to note that charity does not necessarily come from the rich. Shia strive to emulate the lifestyle of the Prophet and the Imams, who gave everything they had even though they were not considerably wealthy.

The Moral Dimension

Shia culture and doctrine give much focus to the moral dimension of our relationships, be it between Shia or non-Shia. There are hundreds of Quranic verses and narrations from the Prophet and the Imams on the great significance of morality.

In praise of Prophet Muhammad, God Almighty says, "And most surely you conform (yourself) to sublime morality" (Quran, 68:4). And in a narration from Prophet Muhammad, "I was sent but to complete the best of morals."[83] The Prophet emphasized that the very purpose of his message was morality and ethics.

There is a narration where Imam Muhammad Al-Baqir describes to us what it means to be a true Shia. He says that true followers of the Prophet and his family are individuals that, "when they are angry they do not oppress and when they are content they do not squander; they are a blessing to those near them and peace to those with whom they interact."[84] Despite the differences in the degree of adherence to the mentioned teachings, this is a general characteristic of the followers of the Prophet's household. Shia are particularly observant of this feature being peaceful and open-minded individuals and communities especially in dealing with others.

It is essential to highlight a reality to which Shia Muslims adhere to and that has a tremendous effect on their worldview. The concept of 'jihad' is often brought up in discussions about Islam, especially in recent years. News pundits have used this term quite loosely in reporting on the acts of terrorism in the Middle East and in the West. Some of this association can be credited to the self-proclaimed Islamists who commit their

---

[83] Al-Kafee: 2/99.
[84] Mountakhab Al-Mawaeth: 186. Shareh Osool Al-Kafee, Al-Masindrani: 9/168.

crimes of terror in the name of religion. They have associated religion with their terror, tarnishing the name of Islam which is completely innocent of their crimes and destructive ideologies. Some terrorists have claimed that they are performing their duty of 'jihad' – often translated to 'holy war.' In reality, this notion has no basis in Islam.

Upon return from a defensive battle, the Holy Prophet welcomed back the Muslim soldiers saying, "Welcome to the people who completed the smaller jihad and have yet to complete the greater jihad..." The soldiers were delighted to be welcomed back by their Prophet but were nonetheless bewildered by his statement. If defending God's prophet and fighting in the name of Islam was not the greatest jihad, then what was?

"O' Messenger of God, what is the greater jihad then?" they asked. The Prophet would simply reply, "The struggle of the soul."[85] In the Shia faith and in the broader Islamic doctrine, jihad refers to the struggle of good against evil. The Prophet emphasized that though it is honorable to defend the faith when it is attacked, it is only to be acknowledged as the lesser struggle. The greater struggle is for one to fight off and overcome his own demons. If a person is to achieve that, he has attained an excellence that is worthy of the Prophet's greatest praise.

This is a principle that Shia scholars and preachers continue to emphasize every year. From educational seminars and conferences to the traditional sermons of the mosques and Hussainiyas, Shia figures remind the members of their communities of the significance of the inner struggle. Mastering the inner struggle is the key to the success and advancement of one's community and nation. Shia culture focuses on this and advocates the necessity for the followers and admirers of the Proph-

---

[85] Al-Kafee: 5/12.

et to emulate him and his family. To emulate the Prophet and the Imams is to be a mercy to those around us.

The Social Dimension

In the Family Circle

Shia culture considers the family unit sacred. After God, there is nothing more important than family. To take care of one's family is in fact an avenue of ensuring God's pleasure with us. Imam Muhammad Al-Baqir narrates, "Prophet Muhammad said, 'In Islam, there is no dearer to God Almighty than the building of a family through marriage.'"[86]

Family members must take care of one another and tend to each other's right. This care goes beyond putting food on the table, it includes establishing an atmosphere of affection, comfort, and stability in the home.

Mutual Rights within the Family

1. **Spouses.** Imam Ali Zayn Al-Abideen spoke on the rights of spouses and how they must observe each other's rights. On the rights of the wife he said, "God made her soothing, comforting, amiable, and protective. And each one of you should praise God for his companion and know that this is a blessing from Him. And he should treat the blessing from God well, honor her and be kind to her."[87] The Imam's beautiful words on the right of the wife are reinforced by the following Quranic verse, "And of His signs is that He created for you mates from your own selves that you may take

---

[86] Wassael Al-Shia: 20/14.
[87] Al-Saheefeh Al-Sajadeyeh: 302.

comfort in them, and He ordained affection and mercy between you. There are indeed signs in that for a people who reflect." (Quran, 30:21).

2. **Children**. It is their right to be provided with the right atmosphere for a proper upbringing. They must be provided access to education and learning. This is in addition to the preservation of their health and safety, while ensuring a bright future for them. On the rights of the child, Imam Zayn Al-Abideen says, "The right of your child is that you should know that he is from you and will be ascribed to you, through both his good and his evil, in the immediate affairs of this world. You are responsible for what has been entrusted to you, such as educating him in good conduct (husn Al-adab), pointing him in the direction of his Lord, and helping him to obey Him. So act toward him with the action of one who knows that he will be rewarded for good doing toward him and punished for evil doing."[88]

3. **Parents**. One of their most essential rights is that they are to be respected by their children. The sanctity of the parent must be protected. It is mandatory for us to take care of our parents, especially when they are ill or in old age. More specifically on the right of the father, Imam Zayn Al-Abideen said, "The right of your father is that you know that he is your root. Without him, you would not be. Whenever you see anything in yourself which pleases you, know that your father is the root of its blessing upon you."[89]

---

[88] Imam Ali Zayn Al-Abideen, Treatise on Rights. Right #24.
[89] Imam Ali Zayn Al-Abideen, Treatise on Rights. Right #23.

Outside the Family Unit

Shia heritage has long acknowledged the rights of others, beyond the family nucleus. Neighbors, teachers, students, friends, coworkers, community leaders and others have rights upon us that must be observed, regardless whether or not they are Shia.

1. **Neighbors.** Many narrations confirm the importance of being considerate to your neighbors and maintaining a good relationship with those who live around you. Imam Zayn Al-Abideen said, "The right of your neighbor is that you guard him when he is absent, honor him when he is present, and aid him when he is wronged. You do not pursue anything of his that is shameful; if you know of any evil from him, you conceal it. If you know that he will accept your counsel, you counsel him in that which is between him and you. You do not forsake him in difficulty, you release him from his stumble, you forgive his sin, and you associate with him generously."[90] While his house was full of people, Imam Al-Sadiq stressed the importance of caring for one's neighbor saying, "Know that he who is not friendly and considerate to his neighbor is not of us."[91]

2. **Elderly & Children.** It is narrated that Imam Al-Sadiq also said, "He who does not respect our elders and have mercy on our young is not of us."[92] The Treatise on Rights discusses the rights of those who are older than us and those who are younger than us. It states, "The right of him who is older than you is that you show reverence toward him because of his age and you honor him because he entered Islam before you. You leave off

---

[90] Imam Ali Zayn Al-Abideen, Treatise on Rights. Right #32.
[91] Wassael Al-Shai: 12/129.
[92] Ma'jam Al-Mahassen and Al-Masawee: 304.

confronting him in a dispute, you do not precede him in a path, you do not go ahead of him, and you do not consider him foolish. If he should act foolishly toward you, you put up with him and you honor him because of the right of Islam and the respect due to it."[93] On the rights of those younger than us the Treatise says, "The right of him who is younger is that you show compassion toward him through teaching him, pardoning him, covering his faults, showing kindness toward him, and helping him."[94]

3. **Friends.** Friendship is highly regarded in Islam and is indicative of a person's character. It is narrated that the Commander of the Faithful Imam Ali said, "Tell me who you befriend I will tell you who you are." In a narration from Imam Al-Sadiq, "God Almighty protects he who protects his friend."[95] And from Imam Ali, "A friend is not a true friend until he protects his brother in three situations: in his misfortune, in his absence and in his death."[96]

4. **Scholars.** On the rights of the scholar the Treatise of Rights includes, "The right of the one who trains you through knowledge is that you honor him and respect his sessions. You are to listen to him keenly and attend to him with devotion. You should not raise your voice at him. You should never answer anyone who asks him about something, in order that he may be the one who answers. You should not speak to anyone in his session nor speak ill of anyone with him. If anyone ever speaks ill of him in your presence, you should defend him. You

---

[93] Imam Ali Zayn Al-Abideen, Treatise on Rights. Right #44.
[94] Imam Ali Zayn Al-Abideen, Treatise on Rights. Right #45.
[95] Al-Kafee: 8/162.
[96] Explanation of Nahuj Al-Balagha, Sermons of Imam Ali: 18/330.

should conceal his faults and make manifest his virtues. Do not befriend his enemies and do not have enmity towards his friends. If you do all of this, God's angels will give witness for you that you went straight to him and learned his knowledge for God's sake, not for the sake of the people."[97]

5. **Students.** Imam Zayn Al-Abideen details the rights of a student in his Treatise on Rights, "The right of your subjects through knowledge is that you should know that God made you a caretaker over them only through the knowledge He has given you and His storehouses which He has opened up to you. If you do well in teaching the people, not treating them roughly or easily giving up on them, then God will increase His bounty toward you. But if you withhold your knowledge from people or treat them roughly when they seek knowledge from you, then it will be God's right to deprive you of knowledge and its glory and to make you fall from your place in people's hearts."[98]

6. **Governor and the Governed.** It is the right of the governed to have a leader who governs their affairs with justice. It is also their right that their governors look out for the people's best interests. The governor's right is that those who he governs obey him within the framework of the law and one's inalienable rights. It is narrated that Imam Ali said, "O people, I have rights over you and you have rights over me. Your rights over me are good advice, the provisions of peace, and educat[ion]... My rights over you are the fulfillment of

---

[97] Imam Ali Zayn Al-Abideen, Treatise on Rights. Right #16.
[98] Wassael Al-Shia: 15/174. Imam Ali Zayn Al-Abideen, Treatise on Rights. Right #19.

your allegiance, advice to my face... answering when I call on you, and obedience when I order you."[99]

---

[99] Nahjul Balagha: 1/80, sermon 24.

Brief Glimpses into Shia History

The Cradle of Shia Islam: Medina

As previously presented, Shia Islam is an understanding of the religion of Islam and not a novel doctrine. Its beginnings stemmed from the time of Prophet Muhammad and the emergence of the Islamic core at his hands in Medina. As the disciple and successor of the Prophet, Imam Ali was the connection of Muslims to him. Holding onto Ali and being firm in allegiance to him rendered one to be Shia. After the Prophet, the central figure of Islam's guidance and leadership would be Ali, hence the focus of the Shia on his personality. A small group of the Prophet's companions, who would be loyal supporters of Ali, became the first generation of Shia – Ammar, Mokdad, Salman, Abuthar. The identity of being "Shia" was embodied in these individuals. Abu Hatem describes that the word was used to address, "four of the companies and they were: Abuthar, Ammar, Mokdad, and Salman..."[100]

The Early Core: Iraq

Kufa

Shia Islam first extended from Hejaz[101] to Iraq – specifically to the City of Kufa. It was a thriving metropolitan city at the time known for its culture and economy. Imam Ali moved the capital of the Islamic government from the city of Medina to Kufa in Iraq upon taking office in 35 AH / 655 AD – this was due to the fitting conditions that would allow the spread of Shia Islam. In Kufa, Imam Ali planted the cultural and intellectual seeds of Shia Islam. He established his school of thought through a selected group of students who were thoughtful, wise, sharp and bold. This group of Ali's students was instrumental in educating the masses on the teachings of Islam as brought forth by the Prophet and his household. Upon Imam Ali's martyrdom in 40 AH / 660 AD, the Umayyads took control of the reins of government.

The Umayyads transformed the Islamic government into dynastic rule that converted citizens into submissive subjects and the advancement of society to a forgotten priority. The oppression, cruelty and hostility they had toward the Prophet's family and the Shia were immeasurable. Their hostility and wrath were directed at the people of Kufa – the hub of the Shia. Muawiya, the first ruler of the Umayyad dynasty, had his henchmen monitor and follow any members of the Shia com-

---

[100] Haweat Al-Tashayo' (The Identity of Shia Islam): 27, as mentioned in the book of Al-Zeena by Abu Hatem.

[101] Hejaz is a region in the far west of present-day Saudi Arabia. It borders the Red Sea, on the north by Jordan.

munity who were seen to be active in social, economic, or political affairs. Those who were seen to possibly be a threat were persecuted, imprisoned or executed.

Muawiya institutionalized the marginalization of the Shia community and ensured that his policies would be executed by appointing ruthless proponents to rule over Kufa. An example of such a governor was Ziyad ibn Abeeh[102], who spared no mercy to those who were affiliated with Imam Ali and his sons. Muawiya and his governors created policies that instructed law enforcement to systematically abuse, crack down, and dismantle any recognizable strength in the Shia community.

Imam Hassan ibn Ali attempted to alleviate Shia suffering and save them from Muawiya's cruelty by retiring from the Caliphate and entering into a peace accord with Muawiya. The peace treaty conditioned that the Shia were not to be persecuted, and were to be ensured safety and security from Muawiya's suppression. This was to no avail as Muawiya broke the terms of the peace accord before he sat on the throne of the Caliphate. In fact, he marched into Kufa spitefully saying, "I will not endure through what Hassan ibn Ali has set in conditions; so here they are under my feet."[103]

Muawiya did not simply rule with an iron fist, he ruled with distaste for principle and disregard for humanity. He established a dynasty that ruled with his same policies for nearly a hundred years. From 661 AD to 750 AD, the Umayyad dynasty ruled the Islamic empire without being subject to even minimal checks and balances or any form of oversight. Their government had no commitment to covenant or treaty, for their rise began through Muawiya's disregard for the accord he made

---

[102] The Arabic word Abeeh means "his father." Ziyad was called the son of his father because his mother was a prostitute and his father was unknown.

[103] See Tareekh Al-Tabari: 6/93. The Amlee Victory: 8/107.

with the grandson of the Prophet. Umayyad rule was far removed from Islam's teachings of justice, responsibility, and accountability of rulers before God and their people. They ridiculed the entire message that the Prophet was sent to deliver to humanity – a message of justice, equality, peace, and prosperity. For the only prosperity enjoyed under Umayyad rule was by those who cursed the name of Ali, which inherently was a curse on the Prophet himself.

The suffering of the Shia continued, especially in Kufa, for the duration of the reign of the Umayyads. The people of Kufa tried to participate in the movement of Imam Hussain, which began at the advent of Yazid's rule. Their attempts were quickly crushed by Kufa's Umayyad governor Obeidallah ibn Ziyad. He employed every form of influence to prevent the Kufans from rising against Yazid and in support of Hussain. Bribes, extortion, persecution, imprisonment, execution – were all methods utilized by Kufa's governor to crush the rise of the Shia.

With the decline of the Umayyads, Imam Al-Baqir and Imam Al-Sadiq were able to focus on the social, educational, intellectual and cultural growth of the Shia community. The Imams gave tremendous focus on teaching and learning. Through their painstaking efforts they produced thousands of students and graduates from Hejaz and the Kufa metropolitan. Some historical accounts have recorded that over four thousand students learned under the tutelage of Imam Al-Sadiq.[104] Ali ibn Hassan Al-Washa testified to the people of Kufa, "I came across nine hundred sheikhs in this mosque of yours [the Mosque of Kufa] and they all said that Jaafar ibn Muhammad had [taught] them."[105]

---

[104] Manakeb Al Abi Talib, ibn Shaher Ashoub: 4/268-269.
[105] Reejal Al-Najashee: 1/137.

Basra & Southern Iraq

Shia Islam spread to the City of Basra in Iraq's deep south around the same time it grew in the Kufan metropolitan. Tens of thousands of Shia lived in Basra, forming a hub that would naturally come to the support of Hussain's revolution against the Umayyads. Like the people of Kufa, Basra's Shia were suppressed, persecuted and executed. Umayyad law enforcement and military guards quelled their attempts at coming to the support of Hussain and his movement.

Nonetheless, the population of the Shia community continued to grow in Basra, as well as in the neighboring cities of southern Iraq. In present day, Shia Muslims make up the overwhelming majority of South Iraq in its entirety.

Baghdad

Significant Shia presence in Baghdad is traced back to the rule of the Abbasid caliph Harun Al-Rashid. More specifically, the Shia population grew in Baghdad when the Abbasid ruler summoned Imam Moussa Al-Kadhim, the seventh Shia Imam, to Baghdad to keep a close eye on him. In and out of prison at the whims of the Abbasids and their fear of Al-Kadhim's growing influence of Baghdad's populous, the Imam was finally poisoned and killed in 183 AH / 799 AD. His grandson Imam Al-Jawad experienced similar circumstances in being brought to Baghdad. He was eventually poisoned and killed at the behest of the Abbasid ruler of his time, Al-Mu'tassim, in 220 AH / 835 AD. Both Imam Al-Kadhim and Imam Al-Jawad were buried in the suburb of Iraq that became known as Al-Kadhimia. Contrary to the desire of the Abbasids, their murders only caused the Shia community to grow in number and hold stronger onto their faith. Though Baghdad has long been a diverse city, Shia presence remains strong in Baghdad to this day.

The density of the Shia population has continued to increase over time in Baghdad, presently making up approximately 75% of the city's total population. Over the centuries, numerous prominent Shia figures emerged out of the City of Baghdad – many of whom established reputable schools and seminaries in the city. The rise of Shia in Baghdad did not go on without challenge. Baghdad's Shia faced mass genocide at the hands of their governors and militant extremist groups. For example, in 312 AH / 924 AD, under the rule of the Abbasid caliph Al-Muqtadir, the Shia suburb of Karkh was ravaged. This attack led to the murder of over 17,000 innocent men, women and children. Over 33 mosques, 300 shops and homes were burnt to the ground.[106]

The City of Hilla & Central Iraq

The City of Hilla was founded by Mazid Al-Asadi in the year 594 AH / 1102 AD. Since its inception and to this day, the city of Hilla is a Shia city. Those who lived in Hilla gained a reputation for their scholarly, literary, and intellectual contributions to the development of Shia culture. A significant number of its residents belonged to a group of eminent scholars that were well respected and regarded throughout the region. Writers, poets, and other literary artists came from Hilla, distinguishing it as a city that was rich in culture and a vital thread of the fabric of Iraqi society. Today, it is considered one of the major cities in central Iraq.

The Shia also settled in other cities in central Iraq hundreds of years ago. To the present day, they continue to maintain a

---

[106] See Tareekh Al-Shia (74-75), from Tareekh Abi Al-Fida'.

strong presence there. One city that stands as a prominent example of central Iraqi cities is the Holy City of Karbala. The city grew around the Shrines of Imam Hussain and Al-Abbas. Over one million people live in the city and millions more visit every month. Karbala has become one of today's most prominent Shia metropolitan cities in the region.

Mosul & Northern Iraq

From 890 – 1004 AD the Emirate of Hamadaniya covered a substantial part of northern Iraq and parts of northeastern Syria. Hamadaniya was known to be Shia in its adherence.[107] After the emirate dissolved, the Shia population remained nonetheless. However, the Shia communities in those areas were met with discrimination, prejudice, and persecution in the centuries that followed.

In the 12th century, the rise of Salah ad-Din Al-Ayoubi (known to the western world as Saladin) brought forth policies that oppressed the Shia across the region. Saladin climbed through the ranks of Fatimid Egypt, through appointments by the Ismaili Shia government that ruled from Hejaz and Palestine to Tunisia and Morocco. Saladin would betray the Fatimids, however, and recapture Cairo (the Fatimid capital) for the Abbasids. With his forces he dismantled the Fatimid Empire in 1171, while in the process persecuting and executing Shia resisters.

Even with the decline of the Abbasid caliphate and the rise of the Ottoman Empire, things were still grim for the Shia. 16th century Ottoman Sultan Selim I made it a priority to quash any strength that was expressed in the growing Shia community of Iraq, as it would serve the interests of the growing Safavid Em-

---

[107] Tareekh Al-Shia: 105.

pire in Iran – a sworn enemy of the Ottoman Empire. In fact, Iraq became a common battlefield for the Ottomans and the Safavids as each pursued their ambitions in growing their dominion and influence. Simply for adhering to the Shia faith, the declared religion of the Safavid state, many innocent families living in Iraq were victims of persecution and execution at the hands of the Ottomans. The residents of Mosul and much of northern Iraq are witness to this tragic history. People who still live in Mosul today have historical accounts from their ancestors on the wells that were piled with the lifeless bodies of Shia men, women and children. Mass graves were dug for the thousands who were killed in northern Iraq, upon which some buildings now sit.[108] Nonetheless, Mosul's Shia community did not wither away completely and continued to live in the city. With the 2014 ISIS invasion and occupation of Mosul, however, the city's Christians, Shia, and even some opposing Sunnis, were forced to leave.

The Arabian Peninsula

Medina, the cradle of the Shia as mentioned above, sits in the Midwest of the Arabian Peninsula – modern day Saudi Arabia. Though the Arabian Peninsula was the birthplace of Shia Islam during the time of Prophet Muhammad, Shia presence there did not considerably grow until much later in history. The Shia of Saudi Arabia are now a significant minority in the monarch state.

Statistics vary, but the Shia make up approximately 15% - 25% of the country's total population. Most of the Kingdom's Shia live in the country's Eastern Province – an area well known for the country's rich oil fields. Though the oil is beneath their feet, the Shia community has remained poor and disenfran-

---

[108] Tareekh Al-Shia: 105.

chised for the most part. This has been attributed to the heavy-handed policies of the Salafi influenced government agencies that have been lobbied to discriminate and persecute Shia Muslims. The strong presence of Salafi-Wahhabi ideologues in the private sector has greatly contributed, in addition, as de facto suppression for the growing Shia community.

The Small Island State: Bahrain

Bahrain is a small island country that sits near the western shores of the Persian Gulf. Its neighbors are Saudia Arabia to the west and Qatar to the southeast. Bahrain was one of the earliest areas to convert to Islam, with records dating back to 628 AD. After a considerable length of tribal rule, Bahrain experienced Portuguese colonization in 1521. About 80 years later in 1602, the Shia Safavid ruler Shah Abbas I expelled the Portuguese occupiers from Bahrain. The Shia community continued to grow on the small island state.

Bahrain's modern day government is a Sunni monarchy with close ties to the Kingdom of Saudi Arabia. Unfortunately, the monarchy of Bahrain has pursued to enact policies that have collectively undermined the Shia majority of the state. Most of the country's Shia are suppressed, categorically granted little opportunity for education and employment. Bahrain's current population is shy of 1.5 million residents – though nearly half of the country's population is comprised of immigrants from Asia. Peculiar at first site, but has been notably observed to be an effort by the state to tip the scale of the country's sectarian demographic. Nonetheless, Shia Muslims still make up the majority of the country's population.

Loyalty from the South: Yemen

Admiration and following for Imam Ali has long existed in Yemen. The relationship between Imam Ali and the people of Yemen dates back to 631 AD, when the Holy Prophet sent Ali as his ambassador to spread his teachings.

During Imam Ali's caliphate, he received overwhelming support from the people of Yemen. Many of Yemen's largest tribes became followers of Ali and identified as being Shia. The Hamdan tribe is one prominent example. Their loyalty was a red flag for the Umayyads signifying Shia expansion into the Arabian Peninsula.

Muawiya took active steps to quell the Shia threat from the south. He ordered his commanders to assemble an army to march onto Yemen. Muawiya selected Busr ibn Arta'a, a vile thug originally from Hejaz, as general of the battalion. Busr's army ambushed the rural towns of Yemen shedding the blood of peaceful people who were caught off guard and in no state to defend themselves. It was custom for a state of war to be declared before any tribe, state, or empire was to wage war on another party. The Umayyads rarely observed such customs.

Busr ibn Arta'a gave free rein to his army who savagely killed tolls of innocent men, women and children. Young and old were killed indiscriminately and even companions of the Prophet were not spared. Historical accounts hold that two of Ubaydallah ibn Al-Abbas' children were killed in the Umayyad ambush of Yemen.[109]

The Umayyads captured a large number of Yemeni women, stripped them away from their children, and exported them like cattle to be sold in markets. If their families fought for

---

[109] Tareekh Al-Tabari: 4/107.

them, they were killed or taken as prisoners as well. The Umayyads were not keen on sparing mercy to the innocent.

Later in history, a stronghold was reformed in Yemen and became a refuge for the Zaidi[110] sect of Shia Islam. Up until 1962, a Zaidi Shia government ruled North Yemen with its capital being Sana'a. The Zaidi Shia community is still prevalent in Yemen today. Moreover, Yemen has witnessed an increase in population of mainstream Twelver Shia Muslims within the larger Shia community.

Above Umayya: Lebanon & Syria

The Umayyad dynasty reigned from Damascus, the capital of Syria. They suppressed anything that had an ounce of affiliation to Imam Ali. Nonetheless, the modern-day states of Syria and Lebanon have been home to Shia Muslims for over thirteen centuries. Historians date Shia presence in Lebanon and Syria to the early days of Islam, as far back as the first Hijri century.[111] In the early to mid 10th century AD, Saif Al-Dawla Al-Hamdanee was instrumental in spreading Shia Islam into Syrian and Lebanese cities and villages. During the Hamdanee era, a number of educational institutions were established in that region. Those schools produced hundreds of scholars and prominent figures from the Shia community that would contribute to the growth of culture, academics and business in their cities and regions.

The rise of Saladin in the late 12th century, however, stunted the growth and prosperity of the Shia communities in Lebanon and Syria. Saladin completed his conquest of greater Syria

---

[110] Zaidis are to be distinguished from the mainstream *Twelver Shia Muslims*. Though they fall under the scope of Shia Islam, their teachings, creed, and jurisprudence is substantially different than Twelver Shia Islam.

[111] Tareekh Al-Shia: 137.

when he captured Aleppo – Syria's largest and most populated city – in 579 AH / 1182 AD. In capturing Aleppo, Saladin's forces ravaged the city and its suburbs in their campaign, which categorically persecuted and killed tolls of Shia Muslims. The Shia communities were constrained and their populations declined in Greater Syria. Nonetheless, they continued to persevere under persecution and their communities grew once again, slowly but surely.

Shia Muslims living in this region took an even heavier blow under Ottoman rule. During the reign of Sultan Selim II, local extremists led by Sheikh Nouh declared Shia Muslims as heretics that were to be killed. The Shia of Aleppo were victims to this systematic genocide that resulted in the murder of over 40,000 Shia Muslims.[112] Those who survived the persecution, fled to nearby villages and mountain towns where many Shia still reside today.

The same Sheikh Nouh was instructed by the governors of Sultan Selim to issue similar decrees against Shia Muslims in Lebanon. Shia Muslims have lived in the Lebanon's north and south, namely Baalbek of the northeast and Jabal Amil of the south, for hundreds of years. The Shia made up the vast majority of those areas' populations. Under Ottoman rule, persecution was on the rise against the Shia communities of Lebanon. Lebanon's northern districts of Byblos and Kesserwan particularly suffered extensive persecution. Such communities were suppressed for the length of Ottoman control over Lebanon.

The worst of these persecution campaigns was carried out by the Ottoman governor Ahmad Pasha – also known as Al-Jazzar, the Butcher. In 1195 AH / 1781 AD, the Butcher was behind the mass murder of Shia Muslims in South Lebanon. He was also responsible for burning down a number of vast li-

---

[112] Tareekh Al-Shia: 137.

braries in the South that contained thousands of copies of rare handwritten manuscripts in various scientific disciplines.[113] Despite the history of genocide against the Shia of Lebanon, they populate the overwhelming majority of South Lebanon, Baalbek and northern Bekaa, as well as having heavy presence in the capital of Beirut.

Evidence of the systematic suppression and genocide against Shia can be observed from the demographic change in many of the region's ancient cities – specifically in modern day Lebanon, Syria, and Jordan. The famous traveler Nasser Khosrow noted in the year 438 AH / 1046 AD that, "Tripoli residents are all Shia and they have built beautiful mosques all over."[114] Today, however, Tripoli's Shia population is a very small minority. Some historians have asserted that many Shia concealed their faith to avert Ottoman persecution.

Adam Metz said, "The residents of Tiberias, Jerusalem and most of Amman were Shia."[115] In the year 420 AH / 1029 AD, the Gatfi observed that, "the scholars in Aleppo issued decrees to the people based on the Imami [Shia] doctrine."[116] Moreover, Jalal Al-Deen Al-Suyuti noted in 364 AH / 974 AD, "In this year, those who followed [Shia Islam] increased and spread to Egypt, the east and the west."[117]

Rise & Fall of the Fatimids: Egypt

The Egyptian people were very fond of Imam Ali and leaned towards affiliating with him from the beginning of Islam. Prominent Egyptians were part of the effort that went forth to

---

[113] Tareekh Al-Shia: 157.
[114] Safar Namah: 48.
[115] Al-Hadara Al-Islamyah fee Al-Karn Al-Rabe' Al-Hijri: 1/121.
[116] Tareekh Al-Houkama': 296.
[117] Tareekh Al-Khoulafa': 406.

lobby Ali in accepting the caliphate after the assassination of the third caliph, Othman ibn Affan in the year 35 AH / 655 AD. When Imam Ali was caliph, he assigned the Prophet's companion Malik Al-Ashtar as governor of Egypt.

In a letter to Al-Ashtar, Imam Ali said, "[Know] that I have sent you to an area where there have been governments before you, both just as well as oppressive. People will now watch your dealings as you used to watch the dealings of the rulers before you, and they will criticize you as you criticized [those who governed before you]. Control your passions and check your heart from doing what is not lawful to you, because checking the heart means detaining it just halfway between what it likes and dislikes. Habituate your heart to mercy, affection, and kindness for them [residents of Egypt]... People are of two kinds, either your brother in religion or your equal in humanity. They will commit slips and encounter mistakes. They may act wrongly, willfully or by neglect. So, extend to them your forgiveness and pardon, in the same way as you would like God to extend His forgiveness and pardon to you. You are over them and your Commander (Imam) is over you while God is over him who has appointed you..."[118]

Through this leadership of justice and wisdom, Imam Ali inspired many Egyptians to not only be law abiding citizens but loyal followers as well. This relationship lasted for years until Amro ibn Aas, minister of Muawiya, was installed as the new governor of the Egypt. Being a staunch enemy of Imam Ali, Amro's administration persecuted the Shia of Egypt even impressing the framework of suppression created by the capital in Damascus. Thus, Shia presence ebbed and declined.

When the Abbasid ruler Al-Mutawakil came to power, he ordered his governor in Egypt to call for a mass relocation of the

---

[118] Shareef Al-Radi, Nahjul Balagha: Letter 53, An Order to Malik Al-Ashtar.

Alid and Shia populations of Egypt. They were displaced to Iraq in an effort to minimize Shia growth in Egypt. Al-Mutawakil made it a priority to reduce the threat of Shia movements by instituting policies that were swift and heavy handed – most included persecution, execution, imprisonment, and displacement.

The historian Al-Maqreezi describes the course of systematic Shia displacement saying, "Al-Mutawakil wrote to his representative in Egypt ordering him to remove the family of Abi Talib from Egypt to Iraq. Following that, the prince of Egypt, Yitzhak ibn Yahia Al-Khatli, drove them out for ten years starting in Rajab in the year 236 AH / 850 AD. They went to Iraq where they were subsequently forced to move to Medina in Shawwal of the same year. Those who remained in Egypt were Alids."[119]

Al-Maqreezi specifically describes Yazid ibn Abdullah's execution of the Abbasid ruler's wishes. He said Yazid ibn Abdullah "followed the Shia and drove them to Iraq and the Alids suffered afflictions during his rule."[120]

In the year 358 AH / 969 AD, the Fatimid general Jawhar conquered Egypt pushing the Abbasids to retreat east. Abbasid dominion declined with the rise of the Fatimids. Under the rule of the Fatimid caliph, Al-Mu'iz Li-Deenillah, a new Fatimid capital was established in Cairo. The following year the Fatimid state founded Al-Azhar University, established for Islamic learning. Quranic sciences, jurisprudence, logic, theology, philosophy, and other sciences were taught at the establishment. For two centuries since its founding, the thriving reli-

---

[119] Khoutat Al-Sham: 4/153.
[120] Khoutat Al-Sham: 2/102.

gious, educational, and cultural institution adhered to the Is-maili[121] Shia doctrine in its teaching and philosophy.

The work of this prominent center of learning was destroyed by Saladin's overthrow of the Fatimid's in 567 AH / 1172 AD. His betrayal to the Fatimids and the establishment of his own dynasty not only destroyed Al-Azhar but initiated the persecution of thousands of Shia Muslims who lived in Egypt. Al-Azhar was converted to an institution that taught its students only by Sunni doctrine – specifically from the Shafa'ai jurisprudential school of thought. Though Saladin executed policies of discrimination and persecution in other areas of the region, persecution was greatest near the home of the new Ayyubid dynasty. The Shia of Egypt suffered the harsh rule of Saladin for years. Marginalization, discrimination, and forced conversion, were all too common; and thus, the Shia community dwindled in numbers. There are Shia in Egypt today, but they are a very small minority – especially when compared to the times of the Fatimid Ismaili Shia rule.

Beyond Egypt: The Africas

There are some historical accounts that have mentioned the reach of early Shia communities across northern Africa and some who traveled south beyond Egypt. However, their traces were eradicated either by conquest that wiped out entire communities or forced conversions.[122] Shia roots and heritage have long been witnessed across Africa; however, the spread and continuity fluctuated depending on the nature of conquest and harshness of persecution by the ruling dynasties.

---

[121] Ismailis are a sect of Shia Islam, also known as the "Seveners." There are notable theological differences between Ismaili Shia and the mainstream Twelver Shia Muslims. Ismailis revere and follow only the first six of the Twelver Shia Imams and end with Ismail, the eldest son of Imam Jaafar Al-Sadiq, as their seventh Imam.

[122] Al-Kamel fee Al-Tareekh: 9/294. Al-Beedayah wa Al-Neehayah: 12/6.

Under the Fatimids, the Shia communities across northern Africa grew. With the Ayyubid dynasty and the return of the Abbasids, the Shia declined. Decline was further reassured with the rise of the Ottoman Empire that reigned for over four centuries and finally dissolved in 1922.

In modern history, Shia presence became more evident in Egypt and the rest of the northern African countries. Today, Shia communities are found in numerous countries across the continent including Nigeria, Kenya, Senegal, Ivory Coast, Tunisia, Morocco, Sudan, and Ghana – all varying in density and percentage of their respective country's total population.

The Sun of the East: Iran

Iran has not always been a Shia-dominated country. In fact, when Islam spread to Persia in its earliest days, the presence of Shia was virtually inexistent. Shia Islam spread there gradually due to a number of factors, the most important of which was the oppressiveness of the Umayyad regime. The Umayyads' racism and debasement of non-Arab Muslims created an atmosphere in the Iranian society that was inclined to oppose the Umayyads. The Iranian people were ready to rise against the ruling regime and rid themselves of a system that discriminated against them for so long.

Thus, many Iranians were at the forefront of supporting the Abbasid revolution against the Umayyad caliphate. Their support for the Abbasids served many and the Iranian people fared better under Abbasid rule than they did under the Umayyads. Nonetheless, when they became privy to the some of the major discrepancies in the Abbasids' application of justice to the people, many Iranians began to lean against the ruling authority once again. The injustice witnessed against the descendants of the Prophet and their followers was an especially influential factor in leaning towards adopting Shia Islam amongst some.

Anti-Alid sentiment, suppression, and bloodshed during Abbasid rule pushed a number of Iranians towards the Zaidi Shia movements in the third and fourth Hijri centuries. This was especially true in the Iranian regions of Tabaristan and Daylam. However, the introduction of Shia Islam began in the city of Qum, which was called Kamiman at the time. A group of Shia Muslims from Kufa immigrated to Qum between 84 and 94 AH / 703 and 713 AD. Some notable Kufans that were amongst them included Abdullah Al-Ahwas and the children of Saad ibn Malek Al-Ash'ari. Shia Islam became entrenched there after the arrival of Lady Fatima, the sister of Imam Ali Al-Rida, and her subsequent death and burial there. Fatima was known for her piety, knowledge, faith, and benevolence. She was an inspiration to many. She was a symbol of true leadership and an example for men and women alike.

The area of Khuzestan in southern Iran, which is predominantly Arab, adopted Shia Islam in the second Hijri century. Many of the prominent figures that settled there were among the companions of Imam Al-Sadiq. The sons of Saeed Al-Ahwazi – Hassan and Hussain – were some of the most notable individuals that were instrumental in spreading the teachings of Imam Al-Sadiq and his forefathers.

Shia Islam would continue to spread through the region including the towns of Rayy that surrounded Tehran and Nishapur in the northeast. Shia Islam became widely recognized during the time of the Buyid dynasty of the fourth century AH. The Buyids ruled over Shiraz and continued to expand until they reached the capital of the Abbasid Empire – Baghdad. Though they were in a position of strength, the Shia Buyids did not persecute the followers of other doctrines even in

Baghdad. Rather, they focused on further developing the region in its rich culture and honoring the scholars who resided there.

The historian Ibn Al-Athir described the Buyid leadership as one that loved the sciences and scientists. The Buyids developed close relationships to scholars and scientists of the state and treated them honorably. Buyid leadership frequently sat with scholars to discuss their research and findings. The Buyids not only honored the scholars but were keenly interested in their work. Thus, scholars from across the region were attracted to the Buyid government that treated men of science and learning so well. They would travel to visit the Buyid leadership from various countries and even write books specifically for the Buyids. The leadership also did well for the rest of its country. The Buyids developed a sophisticated infrastructure for the people to ensure growth and progress. Hospitals, schools, bridges, and other essential projects were developed to serve the public interest.[123]

After the Buyids, Mongol strength from the Far East pressed forward into the Middle East. The Mongolian Empire was known for its grand armies and their vast conquests. In their conquests westward, the Mongols learned more about the religions of the region – particularly Islam. Some Mongolian rulers actually adopted Islam. The Mongolian Sultan, Nicolars Muhammad Khadabendah, is one example that particularly accepted Shia Islam. In his position of strength and his dominion over parts of Iran, Shia Islam further spread in the country. However that was short-lived.

---

[123] Al-Kamel fee Al-Tareekh: 7/406.

With the rise of the Safavid Empire[124] (905 – 1148 AH / 1500 – 1735 AD), Shia Islam took full reign over Iran. Its founder, Shah Ismail, declared Twelver Shia Islam as the official religion of the state. The Safavids were Iranian-Turks who traced their lineage as descendants of the family of Prophet Muhammad. In the Safavid Empire, Shia Islam spread freely in Iran without imposition or force from the government. Even though it was the declared religion of the state, the government nonetheless tolerated other religions and sects, applying a policy of open-mindedness and tolerance as taught by Imam Ali. The Safavid Empire reigned for almost two and half centuries.

Shia Islam continued to shine in Iran even after the decline of the Safavid Empire. The Qajar Dynasty would rise to power and govern much of Iran from 1202 – 1344 AH / 1788 – 1925 AD. The Qajars were also of Iranian-Turkish origin. Today, Iran is the most heavily populated Shia country in the world. Its population of almost 80 million is over 90% Shia.

The Caucasus: Azerbaijan & Georgia

Azerbaijan is a small country that borders Iran's north. Approximately 75% of Azerbaijan is Shia. It is home to grand mosques with beautiful architecture and impressive educational institutions. Its people have a rich history and heritage; unfortunately, the repressive era of communism and Soviet rule suppressed the people's free exercise of religion and culture. The Azeri were relieved with the fall of the Soviet Union. They have since been able to return to the free practice of their faith and have made advancements in the economic and political

---

[124] Ismail Al-Safavi was the founder of the Safavid state and some of its most prominent leaders were Tahmaseb Al-Safavi (died in the year 984 AH / 1576 AD) and Abbas Al-Safavi (died in the year 1037 AH / 1628 AD).

stability of their nation. Azeri Shia are very active in the state not simply because they are the majority, but because they form a vital fabric of Azeri society.

Though the presence of Shia Muslim communities is limited in most of the countries of the Caucasus, the Republic of Georgia is home to a thriving Shia community – most of whom are native Georgians who have had a long history in the country.

Within the Ottomans: Turkey

Shia presence in Turkey dates back several centuries. Much of their existence was completely eradicated, however, during the reign of Sultan Selim of the Ottoman Empire. In the year 918 AH / 1512 AD, thousands of Shia were killed with some historical accounts citing that approximately 70,000 people were killed in a single day during one of the cleansing campaigns. It became clear to the surviving members of the Turkish Shia community that they were to be forced to convert or practice their faith and religious rituals in secret.

Considering the atmosphere of openness and tolerance that is prevalent in the country today, there is a much larger Shia community in Turkey that practices its faith openly. There are nearly fifteen million Alevi[125] Turks who are close in their beliefs to mainstream Shia Islam. Some have suggested that the discrepancy between the Alevis and mainstream Shia Islam is due to the oppression and persecution Shia Turks experienced, which led them to secret practice and away from some roots of mainstream Shia Islam.

---

[125] Alevis are distinct in some of their practices and rituals from Twelver Shia Muslims. Alevis are also not to be confused with Alawites, the groups have different ideological and theological beliefs.

Southeast Asia: India & Pakistan

Some sources have argued that Shia Islam started in the Indian subcontinent. Although these claims are not at all valid, there was a clear emergence of Shia Muslim communities from the Indian town of Gujarat due to the trade caravans that sought India. In his book *The Preaching of Islam*, Sir Thomas Walker Arnold, mentioned that the wealthy pagans in northern Gujarat had good relationships with the Shia preachers and tradesmen that came to their town. The Gujarati people notably treated the newcomers very well. Arnold notes that scores of the Indian pagans converted to Shia Islam as a result of their endeavors in Gujarat.[126]

According to some historical documents, there was a massive persecution campaign against the Shia, both Ismailis and Twelvers, in the eighth century AH. The campaign resulted in genocide of Shia Muslims. The ruler responsible for the genocide was Sultan Taglek, ruler of the city of Bahlee. He wrote in his diary, "Becoming a Shia these days is becoming more prevalent. And the faithful to the government are converting to Shia Islam secretly and I see fit to cut down this tree from its roots. So I ordered the killing of the preachers and the burning of their books and I spilled the blood of anyone who fancies himself a Shia."[127] It is worthy to keep in mind that sectarian genocide campaigns have followed Shia communities throughout history at the hands of militant extremists.

With all the persecution and oppression, the Shia were nonetheless able to establish governments in some regions and territories throughout India and Pakistan. Some of those include:

---

[126] Tareekh Al-Shia: 235.
[127] Tareekh Al-Shia: 238.

i. **The state of Al-Adel Shahiyah.** This state was established in the territory of Bejapur in the year 904 AH / 1499 AD and lasted beyond 974 AH / 1566 AD.[128]

ii. **The state of Al-Kotb Shahiyah.** The state was founded in the regions of Kolkata and Heydarabad in 890 AH / 1485 AD – 1115 AH / 1703 AD.

iii. **The state of Al-Nitham Shahiyah.** This center of this state was located in the region of Ahmednagar, 944 AH / 1537 AD – 1016 AH / 1607 AD.

iv. **The state of Awadh.** Established in 1186 AH / 1722 AD, among its kings was Asif Al-Dawla. He was known to have initiated a watering project in Iraq in 1208 AH / 1794 AD. A river was dug from the Euphrates to Kufa to deliver water to the people of Najaf – that river is known today as the Indian River. After some time, it became a tributary for the Euphrates and from it springs a number of creeks.[129] Among his remnants in the old city of Khno is a beautiful Hussainiya, famous for its wonderful architecture and a destination for tourists from all over the world.[130]

There are other local small Shia states that were founded in India at various times.[131] Historians have observed that Shia Islam was not forced onto others in accepting its beliefs and faith; thus, the people who accepted the faith remained faithful to it.

---

[128] See Al-Masdar: 239 – 242.

[129] Tareekh Al-Shia: 251.

[130] I have visited this beautiful Hussainiya. Its distinctive artistic features include: 1. Any voice, no matter how faint, can be heard loudly on the other side and 2. There are 1,024 ways leading to the path on the second floor overlooking the courtyard of the Hussainiya, which forces tourists to have guides to help them arrive to the path, otherwise they would get lost in its long corridors.

[131] Tareekh Al-Shia: 254-256.

Today, there are over 80 million Shia Muslims that live in India and Pakistan calling those respective states home.

The Mountains of Afghanistan

Shia have resided in much of Afghanistan for hundreds of years and in some regions even longer. You would think that Shia Islam rose from Afghanistan given the influx of immigration there by Alids and Shia who fled persecution in their countries of origin. The Afghans welcomed the immigrants, as they were a kind, hospitable and tolerant society. The Shia immigrants brought with them their experience, trade, and beliefs that came as inspiration to many natives. This mixture left a positive impact on the Afghan people – especially the people of Hazara in central Afghanistan. Today, the overwhelming majority of the Hazara are Shia. There are a number of other Shia communities throughout Afghanistan, notably in Tajik and Pashtun.

Afghani Shia have suffered sectarian prejudice throughout their history. They were subjected to sectarian genocide during the reign of Bajja Sakka around the year 1346 AH / 1928 AD. They were again subjected to persecution and terror with the rise of Taliban in Afghanistan. The Taliban targeted and butchered Shia families across the Bamiyan region. The sectarian intolerance against Shia has eased since the fall of the Taliban regime.

Afghan Shia are primarily Twelvers, with only a small minority of Ismailis. Approximately 25% of the total population of Afghanistan is Shia.

Other Parts of Asia

The spread of Shia in various other Asian countries varies in concentration from country to country. In China, Shia presence is observed but not substantially. There are small Shia communities in the Tibetan region, as well as in some cities and villages near the Indian border.

Thailand is home to a minority of Shia Muslims. Shia Islam dates back to the 17th century in Thailand and possibly before. An account of a Persian diplomat from the Safavid Empire notes that there was a substantial Shia community in Thailand at the time. The diplomat noted that the native king would subsidize the Shia's commemoration rituals during Ashura.

Though Shia Muslims are a minority in Thailand as a whole, they have an especially higher concentration in the country's south. In addition, there are small communities of Shia who live in the nation's capital of Bangkok and its suburbs.

Shia communities have grown in a number of other Asian countries as well. Shia Muslims live in Malaysia, Indonesia, Myanmar, and Bangladesh among others. Nonetheless, Shia have faced persecution and discrimination in some of these countries recently – namely Indonesia and Malaysia. This has been the case when Salafi-Wahhabi funding and propaganda increased in those respective communities – the result being the rise of prejudice, discrimination and persecution of minorities, most notably the Shia.

The West: Europe, North America, Australia

For over two centuries, Shia Muslim communities have existed across the West. The growth of Shia communities in Europe,

North America, and Australia is attributed to the peaceful nature of its people. Shia Muslims are characteristically nonintrusive and peaceable people. They adapt to the societies where they live and integrate within their larger communities. The Shia do not condone isolationism; rather, Shia culture promotes integration and inclusion in their respective communities.

Tolerance, coexistence, building bridges of learning, communication, and dialogue are instrumental to the Shia lifestyle. The Prophet illustrated this principle himself in the inclusion and coexistence of Jews and Christians in Medina through the Charter of Medina. Imam Ali also stressed the importance of respecting, protecting and caring for non-Muslims the way one would care for his fellow Muslim. In his letter to his governor in Egypt, the Imam reminded him, "People are of two types, either your brother in faith or your equal in humanity…"[132]

Shia Muslims have a standing history of contributing to the communities where they live – be it in business, culture, education, academics, social or civic service. Shia Muslims have not only immigrated to the western countries but have raised generations to take those countries as their homes. Professionals, entrepreneurs, scholars, professors, writers, educators, artists, journalists, and public servants have come out of the Shia Muslim community.

Around the western world, there are hundreds of mosques and Shia community centers where Shia gather to worship and practice their religious rituals and engage in cultural and social activities. This is in addition to their active role in public life in the countries where they reside. Typically, they are peaceful and do not cause problems in their interactions with others. As mentioned, this is due to their religious and cultural back-

---

[132] Shareef Al-Radi, Nahjul Balagha: Letter 53, An Order to Malik Al-Ashtar.

grounds, which encourage them to peacefully coexist with others. In a tradition for Imam Hassan Al-Askari, he advises his followers to, "Be a grace to us and do not be a shame to us."[133] In another narration he says, "Be our advocates in more than just your tongues so they see you for your piety, diligence, prayer and charity. That is our calling."[134]

This immaculate inspiration from the Prophet's family has long been stressed by the guidance of Shia scholars. The contemporary religious authority, Ayatullah Sayyid Muhammad Saeed Al-Hakeem, advises expatriates in the West and those who have made the West a new home for themselves as follows:

i. Our most important morals in Islam are derived from the Holy Quran and the traditions of the Holy Prophet and the Imams. The most basic of those morals are speaking the truth, keeping promises, delivering trusts for both the believers and non-believers, and abstaining from fraud, deceit, deception and betrayal. Imam Al-Sadiq said, "God Almighty did not send any prophet but with truth in his words and protecting the trusts for the trustworthy and the non-trustworthy."[135]

ii. Islam emphasizes good manners with all people. We are to treat others with good intentions, give them their dues, and be forthright and pleasant with them. God Almighty praised his Great Prophet when He said, "And most surely you conform (yourself) to sublime morality." (Quran, 68:4) This was also a mark of the Imams from the Prophet's family and they were known for it and as such, they made the best and finest exam-

---

[133] Al-Amali: 484.
[134] Al-Kafee: 2/78.
[135] Wassael Al-Shia: 13/223.

ple. Their Shia and representatives were also known for these characteristics.

iii. You are in countries where the people are used to respecting the law and abiding by the rules. They see you as their guests in their countries. Any time you exhibit respect for the law and abide by the rules, and avoid violating them or deviating from them, you are elevated in their eyes and you impose your personality and respect on them.[136]

Shia Muslims, who identify strongly with their religious leadership, take these words seriously and practice them as such. Thus, Shia are far removed from leaning to radicalism, extremism, and terrorist activities or tendencies. Shia Muslims are usually the first from within the Muslim community to condemn acts of terrorism, as Shia Muslims know far too well the pain and horror of terror. The heinous crimes that the world has witnessed in its recent history have come from the same extremist groups that have nothing to do with the sacred religion. They speak in the name of faith, but know nothing of faith. They go on to kill scores of innocent men, women, and children – most of whom are Muslim. They tarnish the image of Muslims and Islam by waiving flags with Islamic writing and reciting the little verses they know from the Holy Book. Islam is innocent from them and teaches its true adherents to firmly oppose such tyranny and oppression. Shia Muslims continue to be high priority targets for radicals in their campaigns of terror that are motivated by material gain and a twisted ideology of hate.

---

[136] Mourshed Al-Moughtarebeen: 81-85.

A Broad Overview of Politics & Leadership

The position of the Shia towards leadership after the Prophet has distinguished them considerably from other sects in Islam. Both from a religious and a political standpoint, the Shia adopted a unique ideology that informs their distinct worldview. The Shia hold that not only was Imam Ali chosen by the Prophet as his rightful successor, but also that Imam Ali was the most qualified and deserving of such a position. That is why divine wisdom dictated that he be appointed as the Prophet's successor. Shia doctrine relies on several evidentiary points in holding their uncompromising belief regarding leadership after the Prophet.

Shia doctrine on divine leadership is an intricate theology based on numerous Quranic verses as well as chains of narrations from the companions of the Holy Prophet. Nonetheless, the most notable reference within Shia doctrine is the historical event of Al-Ghadeer. The Prophet's Farewell Pilgrimage took place approximately two months before his death. When the pilgrimage rituals were complete, Prophet Muhammad and the thousands who accompanied him made their way back to Medina. On his journey back, the Prophet received divine revelation through the Archangel Gabriel. Speaking to the Prophet, Gabriel related to him the words of God and His divine command regarding the succession in leadership. "O Apostle! Deliver what has been revealed to you from your Lord; and if do not, then you have not delivered His message, and Allah will protect you from the people." (Quran, 5:67)

Thus, the Prophet sent for all the people who had gone ahead to return and gather before him at Ghadeer Khum. On the sweltering sands of the desert and under its scorching sun, the Prophet ascended a pulpit made of large rocks, cloth and saddles. The eyes of the Muslims were glued to his every move. They anxiously waited, eager to learn the urgent revelation he was to share with them in such harsh conditions.

"O people, I am leaving for you two precious things and if you adhere to them both, you will never go astray after me. They are the Book of Allah and my Progeny that is my Ahlul Bayt," the Prophet advised his people. Then he said, "Do I not have more right over the believers than they do over themselves?" They said, "Yes."

He repeated this single question three times and every time they answered him the same. The Holy Prophet then grabbed the arm of Ali and held it up so that the thousands could see. "For whoever I am his Master, Ali is his Master! O' God, be a guardian to those who follow him and an enemy to those who are hostile toward him. Love those who love him and loathe those who detest him. Bring victory to those who support him and let down those who betray him. And keep righteousness on his side whichever way he goes."[137]

When the Prophet descended from the pulpit with Imam Ali, he prompted the thousands of Muslims to pay allegiance to Ali as his heir and successor. On this basis, a number of companions had reservations about the rise of Abu Baker to the seat of the Caliphate upon the death of the Prophet. Though many Muslims did eventually give allegiance to Abu Baker as the new Caliph, a score of companions did not. Moreover, Lady Fatima – the Prophet's daughter – died only months after the Prophet and refused to give allegiance to the first Caliph along with the few who held on to the allegiances pledged at Ghadeer Khum.[138]

This was the first clear political stance for the Imam and his Shia – the few loyal companions and family members of the Prophet. Though his position was firm, he opted for his political opposition to be peaceful –removed from violence and armed conflict. By emphasizing this sort of political statement, Imam Ali established the foundation of peaceful civic opposition in Islam.

For thirty years, Imam Ali's peaceful opposition continued. He remained patient in his principled stand and nonetheless saved the nation havoc and the spilling of blood. With his guidance and leadership from the background, he safeguarded Islam and its community. When the third caliph died in 36 AH / 655 AD, the Muslims insisted that no one but Ali take the caliphate – acknowledging that he was the only one worthy of it. Even after he assumed power, he remained committed to the

---

[137] Al-Sawaek Al-Mohreekah: 42 as narrated by Al-Tarmazee, Al-Neesa'ee and Ahmad.

[138] Al-Imamah wa Al-Seeyassah: 18/23.

people's right to peaceful opposition. Thus, he did not pursue those who did not pay him allegiance or opposed his rule.

Ali assumed the caliphate with one condition – that he would rule as the Prophet did. Though the idea was an attractive one to most Muslims, some nonetheless were not keen on his firm and principled governance. Three separate wars were waged on Imam Ali's government during his rule. Still, even when his opponents confronted him with force, he was never the first to strike. In every battle he fought, it was his enemies who initiated the fighting. In every case, his priority was to avert violence and save the nation from spilling blood. Nevertheless, when the blade was unsheathed and swung in his presence, he defended the religion fervently as truth and victory were always in his grace.

His sons Hassan and Hussain followed in his footsteps utilizing the same form of peaceful opposition. Imam Hassan stepped down from the caliphate to save the unity of the nation and avoid further bloodshed. In the same notion, Imam Hussain's movement against the Umayyads was not one that initiated violence or militancy. Imam Hussain merely refused to give allegiance to Yazid ibn Muawiya, an act of civil disobedience and peaceful opposition to the corruption and tyranny that transpired. He did not rally troops or rise in arms against the Umayyad establishment. His movement was rather civic, civil, and peaceful in nature – from its onset to its last day.

It was only when Yazid ordered the Umayyad army to besiege Hussain and his companions, did the camp of the Imam respond with the sword. Note that it was a response, not an attack. Imam Hussain and his companions defended themselves from the tyranny of Yazid's forces. Their own blood was spilled as a last resort, holding firm to their principles, and sacrificing their lives for the sanctity of Islam. To his very last moments,

Imam Hussain called on the opposing camp to retreat from their position of aggression. Remember that Hussain's caravan was comprised of his family, women and children, and a band of companions. Hussain did not assemble an army to go to war. He did not raise troops to shed blood. Hussain set out for reform in the nation of his grandfather, Prophet Muhammad. He made that clear, but they were set on spilling the blood of the Prophet's grandson because he opposed the caliphate. Thus, Imam Hussain and his companions were forced to draw their swords and defend the faith. They sacrificed their lives and died as martyrs who gave their own blood for the undying principles of justice and peace.

Peaceful opposition was the political signature of Ahlulbayt – something all the Imams practiced. Their tradition is reflected in their Shia and the general political culture associated with the Shia school of thought.

The ethical practices and principled stands of the Imams are also generally reflected in the political demeanor of the Shia, despite the persecution and cruelty they endured throughout much of their history. The Shia are taught not to counter cruelty with cruelty. Shia heritage has demonstrated the honor in restraint and peaceful opposition rather than aggression and belligerence. Thus, they hold themselves back from violating the sanctity of others or from infringing on others' rights. The Shia have known too well what it is like to be violated and stripped from one's rights – it is not characteristic of them to do the same to others.

Perhaps the most prominent touchstone for this, in modern times, is the position of the Shia in Iraq during Baathist reign. The Shia held strong to their belief in peaceful opposition despite the persecution, marginalization, oppression, genocide and mass graves Saddam Hussein's regime filled with the corpses of innocent men, women and children. For more than thirty years under Baathist rule, the Shia did not target and kill innocent civilians that were loyal to the regime. This runs contrary to the behavior witnessed of others, most notably the extremist groups and their supporters, after the fall of Saddam Hussein in 1424 AH / 2003 AD. Militant extremists targeted innocent men, women, and children in carrying out campaigns of ethno-religious cleansing in the midst of schools, hospitals, mosques and markets. Tens of thousands of Iraqi civilians were brutally murdered.[139]

Their campaigns of genocide and terrorism have no place within the system of Islamic thought and the harmony that lies in universal humanitarian principles and values. The extremist groups that carried out such campaigns were not victimized under Baathist rule. They did not suffer from the discrimination, marginalization, oppression or genocide that was endured by the Shia of Iraq. Yet, they waged terror on innocent civilians and caused havoc in a nation that was finally free from its dictator – an opportunity seized by criminals motivated by nothing more than self-interest.

Opposing the Oppressors

Shia culture and heritage have focused much on rejecting injustice and opposing oppression. Shia sources of traditions and narrations are rife with texts that warn against oppression. It is narrated that Imam Jaafar Al-Sadiq said, "Be wary of injustice for it begets oppression on the Day of Judgment."[140]

---

[139] In Dhul-Hijjah in 1431 AH / December 2010 AD, the Iraqi Interior Minister, Jawad Al-Boulani, announced that since the fall of the regime of the dictator Saddam Hussein in the year 1424 AH / 2003 AD, 7,600 terrorists have blown themselves up in Iraq and that 9,600 terrorists have been arrested. In addition, during that period, one thousand ready car bombs had been neutralized.

[140] Jihad Al-Nafs: 272.

Texts from the Imams of Ahlulbayt emphasize their warnings against the excuses of the oppressor and their satisfaction with their own unjust behaviors. In another narration from Imam Al-Sadiq he says, "He who commits injustice, he who aids him in his act, and he who is content with the injustice, are all partners in the injustice."[141]

Shia culture and outlook on leadership is quite different from other cultures and schools of thought within Islam. There is a school of thought that believes in the immunity of the leader or ruler. The ruler is exempt from what would typically be apprehensible and penalized if exercised by an ordinary citizen. Because of this supposed immunity, followers of some schools of thought have defended the actions of unjust rulers. A culture of defending the ruler and burnishing their image by way of creating excuses for their nefarious practices became custom over time. This is unacceptable in Shia culture and tradition. A leader is held to an even greater standard than an ordinary citizen. Leaders are held accountable for their actions and are responsible for the injustices that are carried out under their authority.

Some Shia texts give preference to living in non-Muslim countries, where a resident enjoys freedom, over living in Muslim countries controlled by oppressors. This confirms the significance of the principle of freedom and Ahlulbayt's staunch rejection of injustice and tyranny. One of the companions of Imam Al-Sadiq, Hammad Al-Samnadi, visited the Imam and shared with him a deep concern. He told the Imam that since he moved to a non-Muslim country, people have been telling him that his fate in the afterlife is forlorn. He told the Imam that people have taunted him saying that he will die and be resurrected with the polytheists of his new country. The Imam

---

[141] Wassael Al-Shia: 11/345.

asked him, "Do you remember us and pray to God" while living in that country? Hammad said yes. The Imam then asked, "If you were here, in the cities of Muslims, do you remember us and pray to Him?" Hammad answered, no. "When you die, you will be resurrected as a nation on your own."[142] The Imam reassured his companion that his fate is not determined by the mere location of one's residence; rather, it is contingent on one's faith and practice. It matters not where you live, it matters how you live.

Although Shia history is full of suffering, oppression, and marginalization, Shia Muslims generally did not engage in reprisals against the communities of their oppressors. Rather, tolerance was prevalent in their dealings with others. Their tolerance and coexistence was not limited to Muslims, it extended to the non-Muslim minorities who coexisted with them. And thus, incidents of oppression and systematic persecution by Shia against non-Shia communities have little to no witness in history – both ancient and contemporary.

A contemporary witness to this political tradition held by the Shia are the Shia of Iraq. In spite of the fact that they are the nation's majority population and had been brutally oppressed and persecuted under Saddam Hussein, as evidenced by the hundreds of mass graves left by the regime in central and southern Iraq, they did not carry out parallel reprisal operations after the fall of the regime. Rather, the Shia authorities in Najaf urged restraint amongst their followers and to concede to the authority of the country's courts of law.

Since 2004, Shia Muslims in Iraq have been subject to sectarian terrorist attacks by militant extremists. The Shia had generally held back from retaliating against the terrorist in kind for three consecutive years. After the Askari Shrine bombing in

---

142 Wassael Al-Shia: 16/188.

Samarra, in 2007, the Shia were outraged. Though there were limited reactions from some Shia groups mostly targeting the terrorist network cells and their safe havens, the reaction could have been a lot worse. The Shia community collectively practiced restraint after all they had endured in killing and suffering. Iraq's president, Jalal Talabani, announced that more than 78% of the victims of terrorism in Iraq had been Shia. He also noted that the remaining 22% of the victims were also killed at the hands of Salafist extremists, affiliated ex-Baathists, or as a result of internal conflicts among the terrorists themselves.

Contrary to what some have assumed, Sunni victimization in Iraq has not been due to a systematic targeting campaign by Iraq's Shia as some form of retaliation. Though sectarian tension may exist in Iraq in some fashion, it is mostly due to the terrorists' consistent targeting of innocent civilians from both sects – Shia and Sunni. In August of 2011, the head of the Sunni Endowment Department in Iraq, Ahmad Abdul Ghafoor Al-Samarrai, released a statistic that illustrated how terrorists in Iraq have targeted even the Sunni community. He said that Al-Qaida and other terrorist organizations have killed more than 450 Iraqi Sunni scholars and religious preachers.

Similarly, the Shia of Iraq did not bring harm to its Christian minority either. Christians living in areas with heavy Shia populations have lived in stability, peace and prosperity. They have been, however, the target of terrorist attacks by violent extremists. Their churches have been desecrated and their homes raided. Many have been forced to leave their homes after coming under the control of groups like ISIS. The displaced Christian community was welcomed time and time again by the Shia people of the South.

In one particular incident in 2014, the Shrine of Imam Ali hosted hundreds of displaced Christians. The group had been terrorized by extremists who invaded their neighborhoods in northern Iraq. In addition, the Shia community has also been privy to protecting Iraq's Sabean and Ayzidi ethnic minorities from threats of terrorism. The Shia religious authorities have harshly condemned these acts of terrorism and have opened the doors of their communities to both Sunni and Christian displaced families.

The Islamic Seminary and the Shia Religious Leadership

Religious leadership is viewed as a vital element in the Shia Muslim community. Both a significant and a relevant matter, Shia Muslims look towards their leadership for guidance in their daily affairs. Religious leadership is essentially comprised of the leading jurists of the Islamic Seminary. This collective group of individuals has continued to play an important role in the lives of Shia Muslims, both individually and as a community as a whole. Having a brief overview of Islamic Seminary along with the religious authority that stems from it is crucial in understanding the socio-political landscape of the Shia community.

Definition of 'Hawza'

The center of religious learning that produces the jurists of the Shia Muslim community is often referred to as the *Hawza*. The Hawza, or Islamic Seminary, is an educational institution of higher learning for students and scholars of religion. The seminary enrolls students and graduates scholars from both genders. There are seminaries across the world – the most notable existing in the Middle East. The two most recognized seminaries today are in the Holy City of Najaf, Iraq and the

City of Qum, Iran. Below is a brief overview of the some of the most important seminaries of Shia:

The Seminary in the Holy City of Najaf, Iraq

The Holy City of Najaf is located in central Iraq, about 160 km southwest of the capital of Baghdad. Approximately one million people live in Najaf. It is home to the Shrine of Imam Ali – Prophet Muhammad's cousin and his successor, the first Shia Imam and the fourth Caliph for most Muslims.

It was the gathering place for religious students and scholars for more than a thousand years. Some historical accounts in a number of sources have confirmed the presence of thousands of scholars and students teaching and learning in the old city, as early as 371 AH / 981 AD.[143] The Najaf seminary evolved and developed significantly after the migration of Sheikh Abu Jaafar Al-Tusi 448 AH – 451 AH / 1056 AD – 1059 AD.[144] This is notable growth was particularly observed after extremist Salafists attacked the Sheikh and his school in Baghdad. The extremists burned the vast library he built to the ground and threatened the lives of his students; and thus, Sheikh Al-Tusi moved to Najaf where such a threat was curtailed.

The seminary in Najaf has blossomed ever since. There were periods of time of relative decline when the seminary of the City of Hilla, about 60 km away, also flourished and gained popularity. These periods of shared growth and decline took place from the sixth to the tenth centuries AH. The City of Karbala, about 78 km away, also shared in Najaf's resources and growth during other periods.

---

[143] See Farhat Al-Gharee: 293.
[144] See Tareekh Al-Najaf Al-Ashraf: 2/119 by Ibn Al-Jouzy.

Nonetheless, the grand seminary in Najaf along with those in other Iraqi cities suffered major blows in contemporary history. The Baathist regime in Iraq, especially the tyranny of Saddam Hussein, spared little mercy to the Shia community. The regime especially targeted the community's religious leadership; and thus, the seminary was under extraneous pressure. Thousands of scholars and prominent individuals from the Najaf seminary were displaced, imprisoned or killed. Many of these personalities were grand jurists and scholars that were seen as leaders to much of the Shia community. This targeted campaign of persecution against the Shia's religious leadership started in 1969 and lasted until 2003.[145] At the fall of Saddam in 2003, all that remained in the seminary of Najaf was a meager number of 700 scholars and students.

Nevertheless, the seminary quickly recovered following the fall of the Baathist regime. From 2003 to 2011, the student population grew to approximately 8,000 students – the majority of whom are native Iraqi students. There is also a significant number of foreign students from all over the world that have come to learn in the Seminary of Najaf. Some of those countries include: Lebanon, Saudi Arabia, Pakistan, Afghanistan, India, the United States, Britain, Iran, Turkey, Azerbaijan, Thailand, as well as a number of African countries.

The Holy City of Najaf is also home to a plethora of educational institutions. There are over twenty independent universities and colleges in Najaf. Each of these educational institutions has various branches and scientific disciplines, providing an array of fields of study for their students.

---

[145] There are many publications in the original Arabic language that detail the killing and oppression of jurists, scholars and seminary students which amassed to numerous mass graves in Iraq. Some began referring to Iraq as "the country of mass graves."

The Seminary in the City of Qum, Iran

The City of Qum is located about 135 km southwest of the Iranian capital of Tehran. It is home to the Shrine of Fatima Ma'sooma – the daughter of Imam Moussa Al-Kadhim and sister of Imam Ali Al-Rida. It is also home to an important Shia seminary with a long history. The seminary in Qum began developing in the year 1340 AH / 1922 AD. It expanded significantly during the seventies while Baathist rule suppressed much of Shia activity and freedom in Iraq. With the rise of the Baathist party, the Shia community of learning based in the Holy City of Najaf suffered severely in Iraq. The unwavering persecution led to the displacement of many scholars and students. Those who were not imprisoned or killed migrated to Qum. The Seminary of Qum is currently home to tens of thousands of students of Islamic studies from all over the world.

Qum has grown substantially in the last forty years. There are many religious scholars and jurists, cultural institutions and major religious schools in the city. It is also home to thirteen universities with a variety of scientific disciplines and fields of concentrations. Population in Qum is slightly over one million residents.

The Seminary in the Holy City of Karbala, Iraq

The City of Karbala is located about 100 km southwest of Baghdad. Karbala is most notable for being the site of the Tragedy of Ashura, where Imam Hussain was martyred with his band of champions in 680 AD. His awe-inspiring shrine stands at the center of the city, which became the focal point of millions of visitors and pilgrims. Karbala is also home to a large number of jurists and scholars.

This seminary thrived for years until it was completely suppressed during the Baathist era. The Seminary of Karbala began to revive itself once again after the fall of Saddam in 2003.

The Seminary in the City of Kadhimia, Iraq

The City of Kadhimia is located in the suburbs of Baghdad and today is part of the greater city of Baghdad. The city was named after Imam Moussa Al-Kadhim, who is buried in the grand shrine that the city grew around. His grandson, Imam Muhammad Al-Jawad, is also buried in the shrine. Before the rise of the Baathist regime in Iraq, Kadhimia was a well-known center of religious learning. Saddam Hussein's tyrannical reign ensured that learning and teaching in Kadhimia were eradicated. Baathist state police ensured that the seminary of Kahdimia did not engage in any form of activity. With the fall of the regime in 2003, Kadhimia restored its center of learning similar to the seminary of Karbala.

The Seminary in the City of Mashhad, Iran

The city of Mashhad is located about 900 km northeast of Tehran. It is a large and beautiful city that is most recognized as the home of the Imam Al-Rida's Shrine. The Seminary of Mashhad has grown vastly over the years. It boasts an attendance of over ten thousand scholars and students of religion from various nationalities.

The Seminary in the City of Isfahan, Iran

Isfahan is located about 430 km southwest of Iran's capital Tehran. It is a beautiful ancient city that was once the capital of the Safavid Empire. The City of Isfahan is widely known for its rich history, as it is home to numerous historical monuments and heritage sites. It is also home to a large seminary comprised of a group of religious schools that collectively have a population of over six thousand scholars and students.

The Seminary in the Arabian Peninsula

Modern-day Saudi Arabia has a large Shia population in its Eastern Province. In the cities of Ahsa' and Qatif, an Islamic seminary has grown to provide for the local Shia community that forms the majority of the Saudi's Eastern province. A large number of scholars and prominent Islamic figures have attended or taught at this seminary. It has long been characterized as being a respectable and peaceful institution, like the rest of the Shia seminaries. Hundreds of students attend the seminary in Ahsa' and Qatif, all of whom are natives of Saudi Arabia.

The Seminary in Bahrain

The small island state of Bahrain is home to a Shia majority population that is well known for being a welcoming and peaceful community. This community has a seminary of religious learning that is rich in history. Standing the test of time, the seminary of Bahrain has graduated many distinguished scholars and jurists. It currently hosts hundreds of students under the tutelage of Islamic scholars – all of whom are natives of Bahrain.

The Seminary in the City of Damascus, Syria

The Damascus seminary is located in the suburbs of the Syrian capital. It is home to the beautiful shrine of Lady Zaynab, the daughter of Imam Ali ibn Abi Talib. Lady Zaynab is historically known as the pupil of her father, an eloquent scholar in her own right. She willingly accompanied her brother Imam Hussain in his movement of peaceful opposition against Umayyad rule. She witnessed the gruesome massacre of her brothers and sons, and was taken captive with the rest of the women and children who survived the massacre. She became the voice of his revolution, retelling his tragedy to communities across Arabia.

This seminary, which grew out of the Shrine of Lady Zaynab, evolved greatly over time. It especially grew after Saddam Hussein took power in Iraq. Repression of the seminary in the Holy City of Najaf caused many scholars and students to flee to Syria. In Syria, they were able to continue their studies through the establishment of a seminary in Damascus. This seminary has grown to include a number of religious schools and tolls of seminary students from various nationalities.

The Seminary in Lebanon

The Islamic seminary in Lebanon has a deep and vivid history. Nonetheless, the seminary experienced a range of situations that were dependent on the changes in the social and political climate experienced in Lebanon. In current times, there are a number of religious institutions of learning in several Lebanese cities.

The most prominent of these institutions were built in the Lebanese capital Beirut, the southern port city of Tyre, and in the ancient city of Baalbek. Their educational responsibilities have varied depending on the times and the surrounding circumstances. These schools have graduated many prominent individuals throughout their history.

The Seminary in the City of Lahore, Pakistan

Lahore is the capital city of the Pakistani province of Punjab. It is also the second largest metropolitan area of the country. Lahore is home to a large Shia community. The city includes several religious schools and a large number of Pakistani scholars and students.

The Seminary in the City of Karachi, Pakistan

The City of Karachi is the capital of Pakistan's Sindh province. Karachi is considered to be the largest and most populated city inPakistan. Its bustling city is home to the country's financial center and the main seaport of the nation. It is also home to a large number of religious schools and more than two thousand Pakistani scholars and students. The total population of Shia Muslims in Pakistan is estimated at almost 30 million.

The Seminary in the City of Lucknow, India

Lucknow is the capital city of the state of Uttar Pradesh, India. It is an ancient city with an old seminary. It includes a group of large religious schools and with a strong local base of Indian scholars and students.

These are the most notable Shia seminaries. There are other seminaries in other countries and cities where Shia live, including the British city of London and the Canadian city of Windsor.

The Essential Studies in the Religious Seminaries

There is a comprehensive curriculum for religious studies that is taught in the seminary. The most significant areas of study in the religious seminaries throughout its different stages include:

1. Arabic language
   a. Including courses on grammar, morphology and rhetoric.

2. Logic
3. Philosophy
4. Theology
5. Islamic Jurisprudence
6. Principles of Jurisprudence
7. Study of the Quran and its Interpretation (also known as Quranic Exegesis)
8. The Science of Narration
   a. Narratives, Narrators and Understanding of Narrations
9. Islamic History and Biography of the Prophet
10. Islamic Ethics and Education

Some schools add a number of important subjects, including:

1. Universal Language (most commonly, English)
2. Psychology
3. Sociology
4. Islamic Economics

There are three primary stages of education in students' seminary studies:

Muqadimat: Introductory Studies

At the introductory level, students of Islamic sciences begin the study of various disciplines and acquire a general overview of the topics of study. This stage lasts about five years and it is similar to an undergraduate degree in universities.

Sutooh: Intermediate Studies

This stage of study is where students delve into deeper and more precise discussions with their teachers in their various subjects. Intermediate studies are split into two particular levels: Sutooh Mutawasita (Intermediate) and Sutooh 'Ulya (Advanced Intermediate). Each of the stages of Sutooh takes approximately four to five years to complete.

Bahth Kharij: Advanced Seminars

The intended meaning for Advanced Seminars and Studies is external research beyond the scope of a particular book. The student receives the latest scientific theories from his teacher and listens to discussions between his teacher and the scholars who preceded him. The student must not only listen, but also needs to contribute to the reflection and discussion on the presented topics in a scientific atmosphere free of restrictions.

At times, the teacher will engage in discussions with his top students and may end up changing his own opinions based on those discussions.

The student must dedicate his efforts during this stage and delve deeply into the topics presented by his teacher while referencing various scientifically specialized sources. Many students participate in the studies of various teachers within the same concentration in order to compare and benefit from the diversity of those respected teachers. The length of this period is not specified but it is dependent on the student's readiness and his aptitude for research, deep analysis, and forming his own scientific insight that can contribute to the development of the studies.

Some students leave the pursuit of scientific research after several years in order to devote their time to religious education and social services. Others continue pursuing their research and deepen it to where they reach full maturity in their studies and hone their ability to put forth scientific theories. This is especially true in the field of jurisprudence, where it could last upward of twenty years until the student reaches a level in his education that would enable him to independently derive religious law.

This brief overview clarifies the educational effort put forth by the Shia scholars and the depth they reach in order to become capable of issuing their own decrees and scientific theories.

Some Important Points

Educational Discourse

It is customary in most seminaries, especially in the Holy City of Najaf, to hold student-to-student discussions. This means that the students, in their various levels of their program, engage in discussion sessions about the material they have learned. These sessions are conducted between students who study under the same teacher, as well as students of other teachers. The most prevalent way that these discussions are conducted is that each student takes a turn in presenting a topic or lesson as the teacher would. The student presents the lesson and the other students scrutinize and ask questions. By this process, the students are able to ensure that they all understand the material, fully challenging each person's mastery of the subject matter.

These discussions contribute to sharpening the student's understanding of the topic and motivate him to study more. The student is forced to prepare well before presenting the subject matter before his peers so that he is able to hold those discussions in a serious educational atmosphere. This also contributes to distinguishing the levels of the teachers in the specific topics. As students become more knowledgeable and delve deeper into their studies, they are more able to determine the better teachers for their more advanced studies. This in turn urges the teachers to put forth greater effort in preparing for the lessons and ensure that they themselves are on top of their own mastery of the subject matter.

Freedom in Education

The Islamic seminaries are characterized by their system of freedom in education. Students are free to choose their own teachers. They also have the right to leave that teacher if they do not like his methods of teaching or feel that his level of education is not on par for them. In addition, the culture of educational freedom found in the seminary enfranchises students to have deep and objective discussions during and after their classes with both teachers and fellow students.

Reading Books

The atmosphere in the seminaries fosters a culture of reading. That is why we find that most seminary students acquire very large libraries, ranging from a few hundred to a few thousand books in various topics and areas of study. Some of these books may not even be associated with the student's specific area of study. Students reference these books in order to delve deeper into their own area of study or to enhance their general knowledge. Nonetheless, the culture of learning in the seminary is one that pushes students to read to acquire knowledge above everything else.

It is noteworthy that cities with major seminaries have vast public libraries, the like of which rarely exists anywhere else; the great religious scholars usually build these libraries. For example, there are more than fourteen public libraries in the Holy City of Najaf.[146] The most important ones are:

---

[146] See Daleel Al-Najaf Al-Ashraf: 38-39.

1. **Hakeem Public Library.** It was founded by the grand religious authority, the Late Ayatullah Sayyid Muhsen Al-Hakeem in the year 1377 AH / 1958 AD. It is located near Imam Ali's shrine. This library has more than one hundred branches in most Iraqi cities and outside of Iraq. It contains thousands of original manuscripts of Islamic and Arabic literature.

2. **The Public Library of the Commander of the Faithful.** It was established by the grand scholar and researcher Sheikh Abdelhassan Al-Amini and it is located in the center of town.

3. **Al-Haidary Library.** It is located in the shrine of Imam Ali in Najaf, Iraq and it holds thousands of books in different sciences.

4. **Central Public Library.** It is located in the vicinity of Khan Al-Moukhdarr.

5. **Library of Kashef Al-Ghata'.** It was founded by the great scholar Sheikh Muhammad Hussain Kashef Al-Ghata' and it is located in the center of town.

6. **Public Library of Kufa.** It is located on the road between Najaf and the ancient city of Kufa, about 10 km away.

7. **The University of Kufa Central Library.** This library is housed within the University of Kufa in the city of Najaf.

8. **Imam Hassan Al-Mujtaba Library.** It was founded by the two scholars Sheikh Hadi Al-Qurashi and Sheikh Baqir Al-Qurashi and it is located in the center of town.

9. **Specialized Literary Library.** It is located in the neighborhood of Ghadeer.

It is noteworthy that there are a vast number of daily readers and visitors to these libraries. These libraries offer various services to their visitors in terms of printed books and the latest CD-ROMs. Students in the seminaries and academic universities in the City of Najaf do not typically suffer from any shortage of books. This is due to the availability of vast numbers of ancient and modern reference material in these libraries.

Comparable libraries exist in the City of Qum, the most important of which is the library of Sayyid Al-Mar'ashi. This library was founded by the late jurist Sayyid Shahab Al-Deen Al-Mar'ashi Al-Najafi. He studied in the Holy City of Najaf and died in the City of Qum. This library contains more than a million books, among which are thousands of ancient and valuable manuscripts. The library also has contemporary sections with digital material references on computers and CD-ROMs.

Student-Teacher Relations

The student-teacher relationship is extremely important in the seminary. The relationship is one characterized by mentorship, friendship and openness. The atmosphere and culture of the seminary provide the student the absolute freedom in debating his teacher; in fact, there is an acknowledgement in the seminary whereby a student debating his teacher is a sign of respect and pride in that teacher. The relationship between teacher and student become akin to the relationship between a father and a son. Some Islamic texts have described this relationship in such a manner and attribute the teacher the position of a father to his student. Through this understanding, the teacher takes care of his students and their affairs and resolves their problems, just like a father would for his own children.

Councils and Educational Forums

The seminaries, and particularly the one in Najaf, are rich with councils and educational forums that take place during the weekends and throughout the year. At these forums, scholars, writers, poets, and students of the religious sciences of all levels gather. Without restrictive protocols or formalities any person in attendance can raise any topic or issue, scientific or literary, for discussion and debate. Numerous attendees from diverse backgrounds participate in those discussions, debates or evaluations. These debates last for long periods in a free and open atmosphere. Discussed topics are not restricted to education and literature but they also include social and political issues, among others.

These forums contribute to the growth and development of a student's personality, character, as well as his educational, literary, social and oratory talents. The most beautiful things about these forums are the absolute freedom and the cultural and educational diversity they exhibit. For example, I used to attend some weekly forums while I was a teenager in the early seventies and among the attendees was a great scholar by the name of Sheikh Hussain Al-Hilli. He was the grandfather of the scholar Sayyid Muhammad Ali Al-Hakeem. Sheikh Al-Hilli was in his eighties and would nonetheless participate in the educational and literary debates, with attendees as young as I was.

The attendees at these forums were not limited to religious scholars and seminary students. The forums also included writers, researchers, dignitaries, politicians and figures from various other social strata and segments as well.[147]

---

[147] Some of the most important forums and councils that I attended included:
1. Council of Sheikh Abed Al-Hadi Hamouzi.
2. Council of Sheikh Muhammad Hussain Nassar.
3. Council of Sheikh Muhammad Hussain Haraz Al-Deen.
4. Council of Sheikh Abed Al-Hussain Al-Sadiq, originally from the town of Nabatyeh in southern Lebanon.
5. Council of Sayyid Ali Bahr Al-Aloom.
6. Council of Sayyid Saeed Al-Hakeem.
7. Council of the religious school in Lebanon.

In addition to these forums, there are also religious events throughout the year that bring together scholars, seminary students, and community members. At the conclusion of such events, the gatherings are transformed into educational, literary, social and political forums, similar to the weekly forums.

This culture extended to the people of Najaf who are not students of the seminary. Members of the community regularly form similar forums in which scholars, writers, researchers and prominent figures from the seminary, among others, participate.

Students in the seminary and others living in Najaf benefit greatly from the educational and cultural dimension brought forth by these forums. In addition to the moral and religious dimensions that exist due to the proximity of Imam Ali's shrine, students enjoy a wholesome environment that nurtures their growth. These dimensions manifest themselves in the students' personality, the refinement of their talents and the development of their level of education.

These forums, along with other educational and cultural activities, were eliminated in Najaf during the rule of the fascist Baathist party. Especially during the time of the tyrant Saddam, the regime prohibited any form of gatherings even if they were purely educational or relating to common literature. Citizens avoided any gatherings for fear of persecution by the authorities after tens of thousands of scholars, distinguished individuals, poets and educated people were arrested, executed or displaced. People were very careful, and watchful to a great degree, for fear of being pursued or investigated by the authorities. After the fall of Saddam's regime, the intellectual and cul-

---

8. Council of Sheikh Sadiq Al-Kamoussee.
9. Council of Sayyid Muhammad Sadiq Al-Hakeem.
10. Council of Sheikh Abed Al-Wahab Al-Radi.

tural situation improved greatly. Educational and literary forums recovered gradually in spite of the difficult security conditions still prevalent in Iraq today.

Marjaeya: the Religious Authority

The institution of Marjaeya refers to the Religious Authority that is the point of emulation and guidance for the Shia masses. The jurist that the Shia community follows in matters of religious guidance is referred to as the Marja'. The Marja', or Religious Authority, represents the top of the pyramid of the seminary structure and thus that of the Shia community. This organization, its role and the method for choosing it are quite distinct. The system of Marjaeya is vastly different from what is known about the spiritual leaders of other religions and sects, as illustrated by the points below.

Conditions for Consideration for a Jurist

Shia Islam requires a jurist to meet several conditions, two of which are most essential. One, the scholar must be a Mujtahid (one who is able to independently derive religious law). Two, the scholar must be just. The details of these two requirements are outlined below:

Distinction in Knowledge

To be a Marja' it is not sufficient for the scholar to reach a specific or formal level of education. This requirement stems from the principle adopted by Shia Islam that the doors of jurisprudence and deriving Islamic law remain open. This means that Shia jurisprudence is dynamic and the opinions of prior scholars are not to be held as infallible precedent. As long as education and the human mind are capable of delving deeper and developing further, the doors of jurisprudence remain open for law to be derived based on the proper sources. On this basis, in every age, Shia jurists study extensively in order to reach the level of Ijtihad[148] – an educational stage whereby the scholar is qualified to derive the law independently and debate the opinions of the scholars who preceded him. Based on the maturity of his knowledge and the precision of his scientific opinions in his studies and writings, he is evaluated by other scholars of the seminary. Based on the evaluation of the scholars of the seminary, one may be designated as a Mujtahid, or jurist, whom Shia can follow in their religious affairs and jurisprudential rulings.

It is important to note that this designation does not occur through official meetings or a specified protocol. Rather, it is gradual and unpremeditated process that is mainly dependent on exposure of the scholars to the opinions of the jurist as published in his books and lectures. This informal method gives the community of seminary scholars greater freedom in assessing fellow jurists and their level of knowledge over a period of time. Moreover, the jurist's character, social activities, behavior, reputation and trustworthiness all play a significant role in his following after he is deemed a jurist.

Scholars and teachers within the seminary may have different opinions in regards to which jurist they would recommend people to follow. This recommendation, again, is based on their evaluation of the scholar and his knowledge. Thus, some scholars may designate one particular jurist while others may designate someone else, all based on their free and independent assessment.

---

[148] Ijtihad refers to the independent derivation of law by Mujtahids, or Muslim jurists. A Mujtahid is a scholar who has reached the level of Ijtihad – one of the qualifications of becoming a religious authority in Shia Islam.

The diversity in the opinions of experts within the seminary does not take away from the status or value of any particular jurist. Diversity is actually welcomed and understandable given that different scientific assessments are normal in any study or field. This is why we find harmony and friendly relations prevalent amongst the Shia jurists. This is also due to the absence of any one person having more privilege to a position, or unfair competition above others, as may be seen in some nominations or elections.

Nonetheless, scholars and the general Shia public have often turned to one particular jurist in a specific country or in the worldwide Shia community. That jurist would thereby be rendered as the Supreme Religious Authority or the most recognized authority. The particular jurist would assume such a role without feeling that he is entitled to such a position or title above his fellow jurists. Humility and humbleness continue to be the honorable feature of Shia jurists, in harmony with their knowledge and wisdom.

In some cases, and due to special circumstances such as the support of an authority or political parties, someone who is not fully qualified may be declared a jurist. In those cases, such a person becomes shunned and neglected by the majority of scholars, seminary teachers and by the people.

Shia scholars are distinguished by their high level of education. They spend decades in scientific research, writing, teaching and investing in the students of the seminary who will in turn do the same. A jurist's level of education and knowledge is reflected in the jurist's writings, opinions, decisions and attitudes.

Justice and Piety

A jurist must be just and pious. Justice and piety are conditions that ensure the integrity of the jurist. His behavior and conduct must be in line with these two qualities so that he is upright and fit to guide the masses. In addition, it is imperative that the jurist's positions and edicts reflect his objective scientific opinion removed from his personal interests. A person is not qualified to be a jurist regardless of the high level of study he accomplishes if he did not gain the trust of his community through his behavior and piety.

These two conditions clarify the high degree of confidence that a jurist must attain from the Shia community – especially as a grand jurist. The Shia community sees the jurist as the closest to understanding the Islamic teachings and provisions in which they believe. They also see him as an objective and upright person who expresses, through his edicts and positions, his beliefs of what is truth. His followers in the Shia community trust that his judgment is in the public interest, removed from personal or factional biases.

The Shia are very sensitive to the intervention and meddling of governmental authorities or political parties in the selection of a jurist. They are also wary of any such intervention or influence on the jurist's decisions in guiding the affairs of the Shia community. Thus, the jurists of the seminary, especially in Najaf, are known for their complete independence in their positions and decisions. They are characteristic of not submitting to the whims and policies of the ruling powers. Though admirable, it has come at a high price to the jurists and seminary, especially during the Baathist era of rule in Iraq. The tyrant Saddam Hussein ruthlessly suppressed the jurists, scholars and students of the seminary in Najaf.[149] He killed, arrested and displaced thousands of students and scholars, including a num-

---

[149] See: Encyclopedia on killing and oppressing religious jurists, scholars and students at the Shia religious seminaries and the country of the mass graves (Iraq).

ber of jurists, in an unprecedented fashion of cruelty that is especially reprehensible in the modern era.

In 1984, I had a conversation with a jurist from another Islamic sect. His name was Sheikh Younis Al-Ani, an imam at Amil District Mosque in Baghdad. The conversation took place during our detention at the General Directorate of Security in Baghdad, during the rule of the tyrant Saddam Hussein. The Sheikh was puzzled at the steadfastness of the Shia seminary and its jurists. He was bewildered at how they had not succumbed to the authorities in spite of the pressures by the tyrant to control everything in Iraq. I told him this independence was not free for it came with a price. We sacrificed greatly for it. Scholarly families, in their entirety, were arrested, detained, and tortured. Tolls of men, elderly, women, and children were executed in front of their loved ones.[150] The Shia paid for their independence with their blood and the lives of thousands of their people.

The General Principle of Religious Authority

The general principle for the rulings and edicts of a jurist boils down to wisdom and rationality. In deciding whether to confront the brute authority or to take a position of patience and endure the suffering, a jurist relies on the depth of his education and piety. Those qualities deepen his sense of responsibility towards the public's sacrifice as well as towards the principle and goal to which he strives.

---

[150] Saddam's regime arrested about one hundred people from the scholarly Al-Hakeem family. From the Al-Hakeem family alone, he killed and executed more than fifty people – among them scholars, students, women and children. It has not been possible to find most of their graves for they were lost in the mass graves that filled the plains and valleys of Iraq during the reign of the tyrant.

This heightened sense of responsibility usually keeps the jurist away from emotional and vengeful positions on the one hand and betrayal and defeatism on the other hand. Rather, he keeps in mind the greater public interest and balances between the pros and cons of a position based on objectivity and religious standards.

Those who have followed the Shia movement in modern times have wondered about the secret behind the effective leadership of jurists in the Holy City of Najaf. They have contemplated the reason and thoughtfulness of positions taken by Najaf in the face of extremism and terrorism. Observers have been baffled by the restraint of the Najaf Seminary leadership and how they did not fall into the traps of instigation by those who wished harm for the Shia. Despite the genocide at the hands of the Baathists and the terrorism of extremists, the jurists of Najaf were resilient. They had the trust and confidence of their people.

This same sentiment applies to the present environment of emotional reactions and extremism common across the region. I was personally asked this question during my discussions with prominent figures and in interviews with journalists. In each situation I answered in the same manner: the restraint, resilience, foresight, patience, and sacrifice of the jurists of Najaf stem from the culture of education and learning that every jurist experiences in Najaf. Honing the intellectual and analytical skills of a student is characteristic in the seminary. This is coupled with building a rich foundation of reading and research. On top of that, each jurist was groomed not to be a king but rather a humble servant. Jurists do not aspire to lead; they aspire to serve – as humbleness and humility are some of the most honorable features of the scholar of the seminary. All of these elements contribute to the jurist coming closer to understanding the true Islamic principles and teachings that guide our actions and bless our affairs.

The justice and piety of a jurist enable him to better gauge the greater interest of the community. Furthermore, it allows him to better distance himself from taking emotional, hasty and vengeful positions that could endanger the fate of the nation and humanity. Such qualities also prevent him from falling victim to suspect political forces that are willing to sacrifice all for the sake of their own self-serving interests.

I remember I asked my father, the Jurist Sayyid Saeed Al-Hakeem, about why he would not issue an edict in a specific case. He said, "An edict should not be merely based on a point of view that occurs to the jurist. Rather, it must have a clear and concrete scientific basis. When I issue an edict, I remember my position on the Day of Judgment as I stand before God and He holds me accountable for every edict I had issued. Therefore, when I am not absolutely clear on the topic, I do not issue an edict and I do not need an excuse for that."

The depth of learning and piety are the main foundations that determine the positions of a jurist and his edicts.

Hence we know the great dilemma that befalls the extremist terrorist groups who typically follow the edicts of young jurists who do not even possess the minimum educational qualifications. These "jurists" permit mass murder and the spilling of innocent blood with no educational or moral basis. We find many of these "jurists" are in fact not specialized in the Islamic sciences; rather many of them have deviant pasts and a lack of morals and ethics. These individuals typically have had disturbed and volatile personalities.[151]

---

[151] An example of such individuals is the Jordanian terrorist known as Abu Musa'ab Al-Zarqawi. He has committed the worst types of heinous crimes against civilians and innocent Iraqis – men, women and children. He was a psychologically disturbed

Relationship with the Jurist

The general Shia population looks toward their jurists for guidance in their religious affairs. This relationship is reliant on the fact that the jurist is the specialized scholar in jurisprudence and is upright in his character and conduct. This naturally demands their confidence in him and as they refer to him to determine the rulings of their obligations. This relationship of reference and following is called Taqlid, or emulation. Just as a commander is responsible for his deputies and the troops within his battalion, the jurist is held responsible for those who follow and emulate him.[152]

Emulation is exercised by individuals who are not jurists – those who have not studied and attained the level of ijtihad. Such individuals refer to the learned, trusted, and just jurist. This principle is not a religious position of worship as much as it is an intellectual logical position.

Shia Geography

Shia Muslims are spread across the globe, having an especially heavy concentration in the Middle East and Southwest Asia. Shia Muslims constitute the majority population in Iran (90%), Azerbaijan (80%), Bahrain (70%), Iraq (65%), as well as South Lebanon and Eastern Saudi Arabia. They also have a heavy presence in other areas in Lebanon, some states in India, Pakistan and Afghanistan, especially the central areas. There is a large Shia presence in other countries as well such as Turkey

---

individual and had been arrested in Jordan for his deviant behaviors. He later joined terrorists groups, the latest being Al-Qaeda but was killed in 2006 after his series of heinous terrorist operations in Iraq. This is also true of the terrorist Muhammad Atta who led the operation on September 11th, 2001. His operation led to the murder of about 3,000 innocent civilians in New York and the distortion of the name Islam and Muslims on a large global scale.

[152] Mosbah Al-Minhaj / Al-Ijtehad wa Al-Takleed: 8.

and Georgia. In addition, there are Shia minorities scattered on different continents including Europe, North America and Australia. The Shia communities of the West have built hundreds of mosques and centers where they perform their religious rituals and cultural functions. The Shia are generally very peaceful people who are not characteristic of radicalism or involvement in any form of terrorist activity.

Second Dimension

PERSECUTION

Oppression & Genocide

Documented Mass Killings

The Shia have a long history of persecution, oppression, discrimination and genocide. Over the span of centuries, millions of Muslims were killed simply for identifying as followers of the Prophet's family. Though the oppression of the Shia has contributed to the resilience and patience found in its rich heritage, the pain and suffering this group has experienced is not to be forgotten. Below is a non-exhaustive list of major oppressors and events of persecution and genocide targeted against Shia Muslims.

1. **Muawiya ibn Abi Sufyan.** The first of the Umayyad rulers started the practice of mass killings of the Shia, especially through his governor in Kufa, Ziad ibn Abih.[153] There is a historical document where Imam

---

[153] Historically, he was known by that name because his father was unknown and his mother was a prostitute.

Muhammad Al-Baqir speaks about the Shia's suffering during the rule of Muawiya. In it, he says, "Our Shia were killed in every town. Hands and feet were cut off based on suspicion. And those who mentioned loving us or visiting us were imprisoned or their money was looted and their home was demolished."[154] According to a report narrated by Abu Hassan Al-Mada'inee about Muawiya's firm order to Ziad about killing Shia, "The people with the biggest hardship at that time were the people of Kufa because it had so many of Ali's Shia. So, Muawiya used Ziyad ibn Samiya against them and he then added Basra to his responsibility too. Ziyad would have the Shia followed and he killed and scared them everywhere. He cut off their hands and feet, poked their eyes out and crucified them on the trunks of palm trees. He drove them out of Iraq and displaced them, leaving no known Shia there."[155]

2. **Yazid ibn Muawiya.** He is the Umayyad ruler who ordered the killing of Imam Hussain, his family and companions in Karbala. His army had them beheaded and brought the survivors as prisoners to Damascus. And as if that were not enough, he also committed collective oppression against the Shia through his governor in Kufa – the criminal Obeidallah – the son of Ziyad ibn Abih.

3. **Abed Al-Malek ibn Marwan Al-Umawee.** Through his governor in Kufa, the killer Al-Hajaj ibn Youssef Al-Thaqafi, he committed horrible massacres that are an affront to humanity. Some historical sources mention

---

[154] Shareh Nahaj Al-Balagha by Abi Hadid: 3/15.
[155] Ibid.

that, "those who were killed by Al-Hajaj number one hundred and twenty thousand."[156]

4. **Hisham ibn Abdul Malek Al-Umawee.** He acted through his governors in Kufa, Khaled ibn Abed Allah Al-Kousaree and Youssef ibn Omar, to kill scores of Shia Muslims during his reign as an Umayyad ruler.

5. **Abu Jaafar Al-Mansour Al-Abbasi.** He captured and killed large numbers from Imam Ali's descendants and Shia. Some historical texts mentioned that he used to bury some of his victims alive.[157]

6. **Haroun Al-Rasheed Al-Abbasi.** The Abbasid caliph killed large numbers of Imam Ali's descendants and Shia. He also detained Imam Moussa Al-Kadhim for many years and then killed him while he was in prison.

7. **Moussa Al-Hadi Al-Abbasi.** He practiced cruelty and excessive violence towards Imam Ali's descendants and Shia, rendering the years of his governance some of the harshest years for the Shia community.

8. **Jaafar Al-Mutawakil Al-Abbasi.** A number of historical sources mentioned some of his horrific crimes against the descendants of Imam Ali and his Shia. He had Imam Ali Al-Hadi killed after imprisoning him for a long period of time. In addition, he prevented the Shia from visiting Imam Hussain's shrine and he desecrated his grave and erased its distinguishing marks. The known historian Abu Al-Faraj Al-Asbahani (356 AH / 967 AD) commented on the cruelty and crimes of Al-Mutawakil against Imam Ali's descendants and his Shia. He said, "He went further than any other of

---

[156] Al-Kamel fee Al-Tareekh: 4/285.
[157] Mourouj Al-Zahab: 3/310.

Bani Abbas before him; and that included desecrating Imam Hussain's grave and erasing its marks. He also positioned his soldiers on the various roads leading to his grave so that anyone trying to visit that grave was killed or severely punished.[158] He destroyed Imam Hussain's grave four times in the span of fifteen years."[159]

9. **Al-Mou'azz ibn Badis.** He oppressed through his agent in Kairouan and enticed radical extremists to commit genocide against the Shia. The historian ibn Al-Atheer said of these horrible crimes and the events of 407 AH / 1016 AD, "He killed many from among the Shia and burnt them, looted their homes and killed them all across Africa. A group of Shia had gathered at the palace of Mansour near Kairouan and they entrenched themselves there. They were surrounded by the people and cut off from the outside. They became hungry and tried to leave the palace. As they exited they were all killed. Some others had taken refuge in a mosque in Mahdeyah but they were also killed."[160]

It would appear that such crimes were repeated at the hands of this killer another time when the Ismaili community was annihilated in the year 425 AH / 1034 AD. Ibn Al-Atheer said, "Scholars and jurists praised this great work [i.e. the massacres] whose implementation was overseen by Al-Mou'ass ibn Badis. Poets composed poetry in praise of Al-Mou'ass. Kassem ibn Marwan said, 'they will be killed in every land like they were killed in the land of Kairouan.'"

---

[158] Makatel Al-Talebeen: 395.
[159] Tareekh Karbala: 35.
[160] Al-Kamel fee Al-Tareekh: 9/294. Al-Beedayah wa Al-Neehayah: 12/6.

10. **Safi, assistant to the minister Abi Al-Fadl.** Safi killed Shia indiscriminately. The historian ibn Al-Atheer said about him in the events of the year 362 AH / 973 AD, "He was very prejudiced for the Sunnis and he set fire in several places in the Karkh, a Shia locality in Baghdad, which lead to a great fire. Seventeen thousand people and 300 shops were burnt in this fire, as well as many homes and thirty-three mosques, causing innumerable financial losses."[161]

There were many collective attacks against the Shia during that century. The above was merely a sample of the whole. History mentioned there were twenty mass murders and attacks against civilian Shia, mostly in Baghdad and some in Basra, Egypt, and Qum between the years 336 AH – 408 AH / 947 AD – 1017 AD.[162]

11. **Taghrel beik Al-Saeljukee.** He occupied Baghdad in 447 AH / 1055 AD and waged a relentless campaign against the Shia. He ordered the burning of their library created by Sabor ibn Ardeshir. This library was among the most important educational centers in Baghdad and contained books in various disciplines and sciences from Persia, Iraq, India, China and Rome. Its volumes exceeded ten thousand books.[163] It was all burnt to the ground along with the thousands that were killed.

12. **Abed Al-Mo'min Khan ibn Abdullah Khan, the governor of Balakh.** He committed two heinous massacres against Shia civilians in the Iranian city of Mashhad.

---

[161] Al-Kamel fee Al-Tareekh: 7/336-337.

[162] See the book on the massacres and the sectarian prejudices in the time of Sheikh Al-Moufeed, Sheikh Fares Al-Hassoun, Center of Ideological Research.

[163] See Al-Dawla Al-Fatimyah: 41 and Tarteeb Al-Madarek wa Takreeb Al-Masalek: 498.

He paved the way for these massacres through takfiri[164] edicts from extremist sheikhs. The first one was in the year 998 AH / 1590 AD through which he killed thousands of innocent civilians near the Shrine of Imam Al-Rida. During this massacre, funds and properties of the people were looted. Artifacts and property of the Shrine of Imam Ali Al-Rida were stolen and numerous valuable manuscripts were destroyed.

Many of the victims were buried in mass graves in that area and today it is called "Katlakah" or the place of the killings. This tyrant repeated the abuse in the city and the mass killings of innocent civilians in the year 1006 AH / 1598 AD. He also committed genocide against Shia civilians in the city of Sabzevar, in northeast Iran in the year 1004 AH / 1596 AD.[165]

13. **The Ottoman Sultan Salim.** In the year 918 AH / 1512 AD, he sent the secret police to count the number of Shia in Turkey. Their total numbered around seventy thousand men, women and children. He then issued an order to arrest them all in one day. In that same day he ordered for the mass execution of 40,000 of Shia Turks and imprisoned the remaining population for life.[166]

14. **The Ottoman Sultan Murad.** He instructed his "jurist" Noah Afandi – a young lowly criminal – to permit the spilling of Shia blood in the year 1048 AH / 1639 AD. The latter issued an edict that whoever killed a Shia will end up in paradise. He added that enslaving their wom-

---

[164] A Takfiri is a Muslim who accuses another Muslim (or an adherent of another Abrahamic faith) of apostasy. The accusation itself is called takfir, derived from the word kafir (infidel). The declaration is an accusation of being impure and often leads extremists to validate killing or persecuting such a person.

[165] See Al-Zaree'a: 11/269, as mentioned in Matla' Al-Shams.

[166] See Lamahat Ijteema'yah Min Tareekh Al-Iraq Al-Hadeeth: 1/46.

en was acceptable and encouraged. Following this edict, there were massacres against the Shia and tens of thousands of innocent men, women, and children were killed. During this campaign, Shia were annihilated in the Syrian city of Aleppo where 40,000 of them were killed. Those who escaped the mass killings took refuge in the remote villages and mountains.[167]

15. **Ibn Taymiyyah Al-Harrani.** Al-Harrani led a military campaign in the mountain of Kesserwan in the region of Mount Lebanon in the year 705 AH / 1305 AD. He launched horrible massacres that spared no woman or child. His troops set the orchards and farms ablaze and burnt them to the ground. Today, there is an area in Kesserwan known as "Shayyar Al-Banat" – it is the mountain from which women and girls would throw themselves to escape the attackers who intended to rape them. Even the Sultan Muhammad ibn Qalawun admonished Al-Harrani for his cruelty.[168]

16. **The Extremist Salafists.** A group of Salafists surprised the people of Karbala who were going to visit the shrine of Imam Ali in Najaf, 80 km away, on the occasion of Eid Al-Ghadeer on 12/18/1216 AH or 4/22/1802 AD. They raided them and committed a monstrous massacre against the innocent visitors. The surprise attack killed 5,000 visitors and injured 10,000 more.[169] The

---

[167] See the margin of the introduction of Tashyeed Al-Mata'en: 14. Noah's edict is in the book of Al-Akoud Al-Dourryah fee Tankeeh Al-Fatawa Al-Hamidyah by ibn Abbas: 1/102. Printed by Boulak, Cairo, 1352.

[168] Review: Al-Houjrah Al-Ameelyah ela Iran by Jaafar Al-Mouhajer: 44, citing Al-Akoud Al-Dourryah Min Manakeb Sheikh Al-Islam ibn Taymeyyah by ibn Abed Al-Hadi: 195-196 and Al-Beedayah wa Al-Neehayah: 14/35. Also review Keetab Al-Soulouk by Al-Makreezee and ibn Taymeyyah (Muhammad Abu Zahra): 45. Madafe' Al-Foukaha' by Saleh Al-Wardani, chapter of Madafe' ibn Taymeyyah: 95.

[169] Review the following sources that touched upon the Salafist crimes against Iraqi Shia:

terrorists attempted to continue their attack on the City of Najaf; however, the people of Najaf fought them off before they could reach the Holy City.

17. **Abed Al-Rahman Khan.** In the year 1310 AH / 1893 AD, he launched a genocide campaign against Shia in the Afghani region of Bamiyan. He killed and enslaved thousands of Shia and destroyed their mosques.[170] Afghani historical sources say that Abed Al-Rahman Khan instructed the scholars in his court to issue an edict declaring Shia as disbelievers. Their declaration highlighted permitting the spilling of Shia blood and the violation of their sanctity in order to pacify public opinion and justify his heinous crimes. These crimes lead to the annihilation of 60% of the Shia population in Hazara while others sought refuge in the surrounding mountains. The victims of this tyrant are estimated at more than 100,000 people. He also issued orders to enslave and sell the women and children. The Afghani historian Mala Fayd wrote about some of these tragedies, "Girls and children were sold for a few kilograms of wheat and barley. Each member of the attacking forces bought five or ten women and small girls. There was not one house in Kabul, Kandahar, Gxina, Turkestan and other Afghani states that did not own a woman or a girl from these spoils!"[171]

---

1. The book 'Anwan Al-Majd fee Tareekh Najd by Othman ibn Abdullah ibn Bashar, events of the year 1215 AH / 1800 AD: 257 (printed by the publishing house of King Abed Al-Aziz, fourth edition, Riyad, 1402 AH / 1982 AD).

2. Tareekh Karbala by Dr Abed Al-Jawad Al-Kleedar.

3. Al-Ghadeer, first part.

4. Mouftah Al-Karama: 7/653.

[170] Ketab Al-Taliban: 117.

[171] Review Waka' Afghanistan (Siraj Al-Tawareekh): 300-301 and 345-346.

18. **Sultan Akbar Shah.** Akbar Shah was an Indian king. He led a genocide campaign against Shia in Kashmir where tens of thousands of lives were taken.[172]

19. **Saddam Hussein Al-Tikriti.** Saddam Hussein committed some of the most heinous crimes of humanity witnessed by contemporary history. He carried out massacres against Shia in Iraq starting in the year 1400 AH / 1980 AD through the year 1411 AH / 1991 AD to suppress a popular uprising up until his fall in the year 2003 AD. His victims exceeded the hundreds of thousands, many of whom were buried in mass graves. Over 200 mass graves have been found in various parts of Iraq. Many of his victims' bodies remain undiscovered, including more than twenty-five men, women and children from our family. I have seen, in the horrid jails where I was imprisoned for more than eight years, heinous massacres that included women and infants. We would hear their screams all too often as they were tortured and killed by Saddam's henchmen.

After the fall of the regime, I remember coming across an area of the offices of the general security forces. There was a cylindrical building of a diameter not exceeding ten meters. I inquired about it with the locals. Some of the neighbors in the area told me that this was a basin of sulfuric acid in which the regime would throw its victims.

The Iraqi community recalls the broadcasted images of the regime's military tanks that helped in the suppression of the popular uprising in 1991. The words "No Shia After Today" stood out in bold on the army tanks.

---

[172] Interview with Ghoulam Ali Kelzar, Reesalat Al-Takreeb Al-Adad: 83/106, Moharram and Safar, 1433 AH / 2011 AD, Tehran.

20. **Salafist Terror Groups.** These groups have plagued Pakistan, Afghanistan and Iraq, after the fall of Saddam's regime.

   a. In Pakistan, the militia "Sabah Al-Sahabah" and "Pakistani Taliban" have committed and continue to commit heinous crimes against the Shia community. They continue to carry out campaigns of genocide on a consistent basis. Tens of thousands of innocent Shia civilians have fallen victim to these campaigns, including large numbers of women, children and the elderly.

   b. In Afghanistan, the Afghani Taliban terrorist group carried out repression and genocide campaigns against the Shia as well. This is true especially in the western part of the capital Kabul and the Bamiyan region.[173] In one terrible operation alone, they enslaved about four hundred women,[174] stripping them from their homes, imprisoning them and then distributing them among their members.

   c. In Iraq, the Al-Qaeda terrorist group, under Osama bin Laden's leadership and in cooperation with elements from the ousted Baathist party, carried out repression and genocide as well as displacement campaigns against civilian Shia. Tens of thousands of Shia were killed during these campaigns and millions were displaced. In addition, large numbers of women and children were slaughtered after being raped and abused.

---

[173] See Taliban: 128.
[174] See Al-Masdar: 127.

The Jordanian Abu Musa'ab Al-Zarqawi was the cruelest field commander and the thirstiest for the blood of the innocent. On the Baathist side, the criminal acts were committed by two groups, that of Izzat Al-Douri, assistant to Saddam, and Younis Al-Ahmad. Other criminal extremist groups also contributed to these campaigns, including "the Iraqi Islamic Republic," "the Twentieth Revolutionary Brigades," "The Army of the Sunna People," "Omar's Corps," "The Army of the Naqshbandi Movement," and "the Islamic Army," among others.

It should be noted that there is a close alliance between these extremist groups and elements of Saddam's repressive regime. In fact, many of the leaders and members of these terrorist organizations were part of the Saddam's Baathist regime.

We note from this quick review of massacres and genocide the extent of the suffering and sectarian persecution experienced by the Shia. This oppression continues to happen today where one finds mass killings occurring almost on a daily basis in Iraq, Pakistan and Afghanistan, among other countries. This is in addition to the oppression and marginalization experienced by Shia in a number of other countries. All of this is happening and much of the world has turned a blind eye. From government to international humanitarian organizations, there is little said or done in opposition to the oppression of Shia Muslims. No country or group today is facing what the Shia continue to endure through attacks and mass killings at the hands of militant extremists.

It is noteworthy to mention that the heinous crimes committed are not limited to extremist militant groups, but are also funded and supported by dictatorial regimes that essentially believe in no religion. The Shia are the most targeted faith-based group in the world. Nevertheless, their patience and determination to hold on to their identity and faith are nothing less than admirable. Their strength is found in their rooted culture, which has enabled them to persevere and maintain their identity while other nations have crumbled under much less pressure and persecution.

I pray that the consortium of international humanitarian efforts and the work of those with a conscience come together in cooperation and collaboration. Let them come together to spread the culture of dialogue and peaceful coexistence between communities, people and nations around the globe.

The Most Significant Motives for Genocide

The Political Motive

Many of the repression and genocide campaigns suffered by the Shia were politically motivated. Many of the dictatorial regimes that ordered such campaigns designed them to further their plans motivated by their own selfish interests.

These regimes took advantage of the sectarian differences within the greater Muslim community to stir controversy with their followers. Their aim was to transform the ideological differences into a justification for fighting and mass killings. These regimes committed their crimes under the sectarian and religious guises to ensure public support and prevent the emergence of an effective opposition from both within and without the Shia community.

Dictator regimes frequently employ twisted and indirect methods to support terrorist groups for the purpose of implementing their racist and sectarian agendas. This has been especially the case in the present day in order to avoid international condemnation by other countries and international and humanitarian organizations. Nonetheless, countries that promote terrorism cannot conceal their support and sponsorships in every way due to the increase of witnesses and evidence that have piled up over the years. Some evidentiary points include:

1. The financial resources owned by these extremist terrorist groups are not in alignment with the theory of grass roots financing. Most of the followers and supporters of these terrorist organizations tend to be poor uneducated communities. Take for example the recording broadcast by Al-Jazeera for the terrorist Abu Musa'ab Al-Zarqawi – the former leader of Al-Qaeda in Iraq. In that broadcast, he stated that preparing, setting up and exploding each explosive vehicle in Iraq cost approximately $600,000. This operational cost was prior to the establishment of permanent bases for Al-Qaeda in Iraq.

2. Terrorist organizations operating at such a high level have high costs in operations. From salaries to equipment and weapons, they cannot be making all their payments with bags of cash. It only follows that they would have bank accounts for money flow. The stringent international banking system does not allow for the transfer of funds between countries without clear justification. This indicates that these groups are being supported by countries that are providing them with the official pretenses for transferring vast amounts of funds and facilitating their escape from international oversight.

3. The intense media support for these groups provided by influential Arabic channels which are owned by states with obscene wealth.

4. The evident differences in the practices of the extremist terrorist groups confirm their association with specific political plans, removed from the motive of pure religious extremism. For example, we find that the terrorist Taliban organization in Pakistan has assumed genocide campaigns against civilian Shia as a primary goal for itself. In the meantime, this is not clear for the Afghani Taliban group and this is in spite of the fact that the two groups follow the same religious ideology. This confirms that each of these groups is carrying out the interests and plans of the dictatorial regimes that support them regardless of the sectarian differences with the Shia.

The Ideological Motive

Salafist ideology has become a suitable platform for those who carry out genocide and persecution of religious minorities, particularly the Shia. Radicalism, rejection of others, hate, militancy, and the violation of sacred places are all characteristics of Salafism. The militant Salafist culture has become the perfect malleable tool for dictatorial regimes to drive their own narrow self-interests.

Note that Shia Muslims and Muslims from other schools of thought do have ideological differences. However, those differences are minute in the greater scheme of things. This extremist culture that feeds its followers the notion of opposing Shia, violating their rights and sanctities, and persecuting them does not coincide with any Islamic teachings. No level-minded mainstream scholar from any sect of Islam has ever justified such brutal campaigns of oppression.

An objective view of these crimes will show the saturation of hate and ignorance that has come forth from this extremist culture that only advocates rejection and violence. This advocacy points are primary drivers for the genocide campaigns in the areas where these groups are active.

The true and customary culture of Sunni Muslims does not correspond at all with these deviant beliefs. The clear proof of this is their peaceful coexistence in all countries where the two groups live together, along with other sects and religions. This includes Pakistan prior to the infiltration of the Taliban and its Salafist culture there. Even Afghanistan has seen a reduction of sectarian terrorist acts after the removal of the Taliban regime – proving the influence of that culture on the turn of events in the country.

The culture of hate and eradicating the 'other' is characteristic of the extremist Salafist groups. This culture has spread to influence other groups and even moderate powers. The heinous crimes of affiliated extremist groups in Algeria against native moderate Sunni civilians subjugated almost 200,000 victims in the 1990s.

These groups have committed violent crimes similar to those committed against Shia, particularly after their influence and reach had expanded to some western countries. Subsequent events in the last three decades have shown the similarities and distinctions between their bloody practices and the practices of other terrorist groups that are active in those countries.

Implications of the Global Danger of Extremism

The dangers of extremism and terrorism are not limited to specific countries or communities. Rather, their impact is gradually extending to other communities and countries around the globe. The modern world is interdependent and more connected than ever. The world has basically become one large unified town, and its neighborhoods and regions interact and react to what is happening. The dangers terrorists pose and the culture of extremism and hatred they carry are not limited to criminal acts against peaceful and stable societies. Rather, this provides the suitable atmosphere to grow the extremist culture among people and communities who gradually come to believe that their moderation did not provide them with security and peace.

That is why we notice the gradual growth of extremism in some western communities as it is a reaction to the Wahhabi extremism. Evidence of this is the massacre perpetrated in Oslo by Anders Behring Breivik and his eagerness to prove his mental capacity in court. This is in addition to the issuance of statements of support for him by extremist groups in several European countries. Furthermore, continued attacks on Islamic holy places and unjustified provocative practices all provide a platform for polarization, hatred and militancy instead of a culture of tolerance and peaceful coexistence.

The brief points discussed above illustrate why this culture is considered one of the most dangerous cultures threatening our stability and peace of our global society. It is therefore incumbent on all of our communities and their various organizations to find effective solutions to address this culture and to limit its negative effects.

Third Dimension
HORIZONS

Prospects for the Future

The global Shia community is a key player in the advancement of humanity with a vital role in the prosperity of our world as a whole. Given their unique characteristics and features, the Shia will have a prosperous future and an active role both on the Islamic and general humanitarian fronts. This is especially true after the fall of the oppressive regime of Saddam Hussein in Iraq. However, this is contingent on a number of commitments and serious steps that are required. The most important of which are:

1. The ability of Shia to reflect the rationality of Islam and its alignment with logic on one hand, and its human and moral dimensions on the other hand.

2. The Shia must possess that which develops and deepens their spirituality and sense of security. This can be achieved through careful observation and thoughtfulness, contemplation, and dedication to worship. This will embolden one's spiritual side. Strong spirituality gives a person the tranquility and stability to persevere

through the hurdles of the harsh arena of life. It is something that the modern culture of materialism continues to lack.

3. They need diligence and the ability to adapt to the difficulties born out of their severe suffering over centuries. The Shia need to hold on to their culture of patience and resilience that has become the trademark of the Shia personality. If adopted properly it can be a positive element for nations and people in the face of the difficulty and tragedy. With such resolve, havoc, ruin, and collapse of communities are mitigated or prevented all together.

4. The principle of peaceful coexistence and openness with those who oppose them is a principle that has been clearly reflected in societies where Shia mix with others. Therefore, we find that the religious and sectarian minorities that coexist with Shia feel safe and secure and in fact, have close relationships with them. Christians and Sabeans in southern Iraq did not suffer any harm or displacement like others did in non-Shia areas. Even Shia living in southern Iraq did not suffer as badly as those who lived in western Iraq, Mosul, and some areas of Baghdad. Genocide and displacement at the hands of extremists hit the Shia in those areas the worst. That suffering was in spite of the fact that Shia represent the majority and the stronger side of the population in Iraq after the fall of Saddam's regime.

5. The principle of Ijtihad must remain alive. This principle is the basis of Shia doctrine, giving it vitality and dynamism that make the Shia school of thought more in line with the evolving and ever-changing reality. This is a key factor in the open-mindedness and logic

of Shia Islam and its distinction from extremism, rigidity, intolerance and violence.

Sense of Value in the Shia Identity

1. **There must be an acknowledgment of value in the Shia identity.** The continuance of successive oppression throughout time has crushed the personality of the oppressed; thus, individuals and communities become blinded to their own self-worth. Lacking self-worth, people tend to be meeker and more submissive as opposed to standing up for their rights. This in turn, encourages the oppressors to continue in their acts of oppression and genocidal campaigns. Throughout history, the Shia have been subjected to practices of marginalization and collective oppression. Thus, it is necessary for Shia to reevaluate these past incidents.

    Even though many of the mass killings of the past and present were a result of harsh conditions imposed on them, some of these occurrences were not necessarily as such. In some situations, the Shia could have prevented the negative outcomes they faced by being more assertive and aware of their own worth and freedom. There is plenty of proof for that in the sectarian genocide campaigns that occurred in Iraq after the fall of Saddam in 2003. Even former Iraqi president Jalal Al-Talabani said that 78% of terror victims in Iraq were Shia while the terrorists were a small minority. Furthermore, the organized campaigns of mass displacement that affected millions of Shia were carried out by terrorists and the remnants of the Baathist regime – both collectively did not possess a high level of power or dominion. These tragedies could have been mitigated if the Shia had greater awareness of their own self-worth and were stouter in their positions. Had that been the case, it would have limited the number of innocent victims significantly.

Once again, we reaffirm that Shia are currently facing a true test to deepen their sense of self-worth firstly and to impose respect for themselves by others secondly, just as they respect the rights of others. This would provide the proper ground and atmosphere in their journey towards the future.

Clarity of Identity

2. **Clarity of identity**, goal setting and working towards those goals are things that many Shia communities demand. A number of communities have suffered from confusion and vagueness as a result of various external pressures and marginalization in many of their countries. Coupled with extensive media campaigns undertaken by those who have animosity toward the Shia, some members of the Shia community have lived in a state of confusion or lack of direction. Even worse, some may have misperceived or completely lost their identity. Thus, it is essential to work on initiatives for education and awareness of Shia's rich heritage and noble identity.

Serious Contributions to Countries and Communities

3. **Serious contributions to the construction of their countries and communities.** In addition, the transition from the margins of society, which was forced upon them, to

having an active, effective and positive role in the greater community. This is aided by large numbers of those with competencies and specialties in the various fields of science and management. It will especially be so after their gradual recognition and the emergence of their role both regionally and globally. This requires them to seriously develop themselves, individually and as communities. The Shia are to take it upon themselves to delve deeper in various disciplines that are needed in their local communities and in the global community as well.

Decision-Making and Civilized Societies

4. **Being confidently open to the centers of decision-making and civilized societies.** The Shia community is to bypass and transcend beyond the bands of control and effects of terror imposed on them by sectarian dictatorial powers and extremist groups. They are to break free from this grip that has imprisoned them for centuries. In that spirit, they are to engage with the world centers of policy and decision-making. This same openness and interaction with these communities contribute to a greater extent to reducing the pressure of extremists, especially in today's interconnected world.

Logic and Passion

5. **Delicate intermingling between rationality and emotion.** Through the balance of logic and passion, the Shia will be preserving the proper role for each in its respective fields and without hyperbole or failure of the

other. Rationality and logic would have the role of guidance, and passion and emotion would have the role of motivation and renewed energy. This includes an emphasis on dealing with issues and confrontations in our society in a logical and pragmatic manner. We should employ all of the associated scientific, cultural and economic dimensions and save our communities from empty rhetoric and loaded slogans.

Interacting Wisely and Responsibly

6. **Interacting wisely and with the utmost responsibility.** This is especially crucial on the part of the community's leadership and elite, with the challenges that lie ahead and their ramifications. Also, avoiding confusion, emotional reactions, or becoming pre-occupied with personal or factional gains at the expense of public interest is essential. This is especially important in light of the domestic and regional changes in the Arab and Islamic worlds. These changes could have an impact on the whole world. It is vital to keep close observation and consideration for all the changing conditions and emerging elements regionally and globally. There should be a clear watch and distinction between friends, enemies and those who assume to be neutral.

The Shia's investment in the above characteristics, along with taking into account the observations we noted, could make their culture and community an effective factor and a positive element of global prosperity and advancement.

God willing, I hope this is realized and achieved.

Riyadh Al-Hakeem

The Holy City of Najaf

INDEX

IMAGES

Attack on the Askari Shrine

The Askari Shrine is the burial site of 10th and 11th Imams, Imam Ali Al-Hadi and Imam Hassan Al-Askari. This image was taken after the terrorist attack on the shrine in 2006.

The Askari Shrine

This is the Askari Shrine, known for its magnificent golden dome, before it was attacked by terrorists in 2006.

The Grand Mosque

The Grand Mosque, built around the Holy Kaaba, in the Holy City of Mecca in Hejaz – modern day Saudi Arabia.

The Prophet's Mosque

The Shrine of the Holy Prophet Muhammad, also known as the Prophet's Mosque is located in the Holy City of Medina in Hejaz – modern day Saudi Arabia.

Imam Ali Shrine

The Shrine of Imam Ali in the Holy City of Najaf, Iraq. The Shrine was built on around the burial site of Imam Ali and developed into one of the holiest pilgrimage sites for Shia Muslims worldwide.

The Baqee Cemetery

The Baqee Cemetery is the burial site of four Imams: Imam Hassan ibn Ali, Imam Ali Zayn Al-Abideen, Imam Muhammad Al-Baqir, and Imam Jaafar Al-Sadiq. The graves were held under a domed shrine for many years until the shrine was demolished on April 21, 1925 by Saudi authorities.

The Baqee Shrine

Before being destroyed in 1925 by Saudi authorities, this shrine stood as a visitation site for Muslim pilgrims. The Baqee Shrine was home to the four Imams: Imam Hassan ibn Ali, Imam Ali Zayn Al-Abideen, Imam Muhammad Al-Baqir, and Imam Jaafar Al-Sadiq.

Damage to the Shrine of Imam Hussain

This image depicts the damage that was done to the shrine of Imam Hussain during the attacks of the Baathist Regime in 1991.

Imam Hussain Shrine

The Shrine of Imam Hussain in Karbala, Iraq. The shrine was
built on the land of Karbala where the Imam was killed along
with sons, brothers, and companions on the Day of Ashura.

The Kadhimiya Shrine

The Kadhimiya Shrine in Baghdad, Iraq is the burial site of the seventh and ninth Imams: Imam Moussa Al-Kadhim and his grandson Imam Muhammad Al-Jawad.

Imam Al-Rida Shrine

The Shrine of Imam Ali Al-Rida is located in Mashhad, Iran.
Imam Al-Rida is the eighth Imam.

The Grand Mosque of Kufa

It was in this mosque that Imam Ali led prayers while assuming the role of leadership of the Muslim nation as Caliph. It was in this mosque that he was assassinated while offering the dawn prayers during the Holy Month of Ramadan.

The Shrine of Abbas ibn Ali

Abbas ibn Ali, the brother of Imam Hussain, was murdered alongside his brother during the tragedy of Karbala. This shrine marks his burial site, less than 500 meters from the shrine of his brother.

The Shrine of Zaynab bint Ali

The shrine of Lady Zaynab stands tall in the city of Damascus, where she was once taken as prisoner after the tragedy of Karbala. Terror groups have threatened to destroy her shrine specifically, along with all other similar sites.

Millions March towards the Shrine

This image captures only a fraction of the millions that march on to visit the Shrine of Imam Hussain in Karbala, Iraq during the Arbaeen (the 40th Day after the commemoration of the Day of Ashura).

Mass Graves by Saddam Hussein

Iraqi policemen inspect human remains at a mass grave uncovered in the desert of Diwaniyah province, some 130 km south of Baghdad, Iraq, 10 July 2011. Iraqi authorities uncovered a mass grave with 800 corpses near the central city of Diwaniyah. Officials said that the remains are believed to be Iraqis killed during the rule of ousted leader Saddam Hussein, it is one of the bigger mass graves unearthed in recent years.

Hawza Students Studying

The images above show different study group sessions of Hawza students in the Holy City of Najaf.

Al-Faydeeyah Seminary

Located in the City of Qum, Iran, Al-Faydeeyah Seminary is a school for higher religious learning in one of Iran's largest seminary cities.

Zahra University

The robust institute for higher education, Zahra University is located in Qum, Iran.

The Hakeem Public Library

This image is a view of the interior of the Hakeem Public Library in the Holy City of Najaf, Iraq.

The Library of Sayyid Al-Mar'ashi

This image is taken of the interior of the vast Sayyid Al-Mar'ashi Library in the City of Qum, Iran.

Johann Wolfgang von Goethe

In his writings on the Tragedy of Karbala, the German Philosopher Goethe has been quoted to call Imam Hussain, "the Body of Human Conscience."

Washington Irving

Known as the "first American man of letters," Washington Irving praised Imam Ali as the noblest branch of the Qureish tribe and one who "possessed the three qualities most prized by Arabs: courage, eloquence, and munificence."

Thomas Carlyle

The Scottish writer admired Imam Ali saying, "Something chivalrous in him; brave as a lion; yet with a grace, a truth and affection worthy of Christian knighthood."

Bertrand Russell

The British philosopher expressed pride in Imam Hussain saying, "Humanity should be proud of Hussain who exploded the largest volcano and uprooted the tyrannical rulers who oppressed their people."

Saddam Hussein

This image of Saddam Hussein was taken during his criminal trial in which he and his aides were charged and convicted of war crimes, crimes against humanity, and genocide. Under his rule hundreds of thousands of Kurdish and Shiite Iraqis were put to death.

Abu Musa'ab Al-Zarqawi

Abu Musa'ab Al-Zarqawi was a Jordan national that led the Al-Qaeda branch in Iraq and was responsible for many of the terrorist attacks on Iraqi civilians, particularly Shiites, from 2003 to 2006.

Abu Bakr Al-Baghdadi

The current leader of the terrorist organization Daesh (ISIS), Abu Bakr Al-Baghdadi, has rallied his band of terrorists to target Shiite civilians in Iraq, Syria, Lebanon and across the Middle East. His tactics were deemed so extreme that even Al-Qaeda has dissociated from Baghdadi and his organization.

Genocide in Iraq

The first image depicts the Camp Speicher massacre in which over 1,500 unarmed Iraqi servicemen were captured and executed by ISIS. The second image depicts dead Ayzidi children also killed by ISIS.

Die Pforte der Weisheit

Von Friedrich Rückert

Weil der Prophet (s.) gesprochen hat:

Ich bin die Stadt der Weisheit, Ali aber ist die Pforte,
so wollten, die sich ärgerten am Worte, Abtrünnige
von Anzahl zehn, die Proben solcher Weisheit sehn.

Sie sprachen: Lasst uns jeder einzeln fragen, und
wird er jedem gleiche Antwort sagen, und jedem mit
verschiednem Worte, so soll er sehn der Weisheit
Pforte, ob andern Gütern vorzuzieh'n die Weisheit sei,
as fraget ihn.

Und als ihn so der erste fragte, war dies das Wort
das Ali sagte:

Goethe's Writings on Imam Ali

Writings of the German philosopher and author Goethe about
the wisdom of Imam Ali.

UNITED NATIONS DEVELOPMENT PROGRAMME
ARAB FUND FOR ECONOMIC AND SOCIAL DEVELOPMENT

ARAB HUMAN DEVELOPMENT REPORT 2002

Creating Opportunities for Future Generations

Arab Human Development Report 2002

The UN's Arab Human Development Report in 2002 cited to Imam Ali and his principles on governance. The report advised Arab nations to use the teachings of Imam Ali as a guide for good and just governance.

BOX 7.3

Imam Ali bin abi Taleb: on governance

• He who has appointed himself an Imam of the people must begin by teaching himself before teaching others, his teaching of others must be first by setting an example rather than with words, for he who begins by teaching and educating himself is more worthy of respect than he who teaches and educates others.

• Your concern with developing the land should be greater than your concern with collecting taxes, for the latter can only be obtained by developing; whereas he who seeks revenue without development destroys the country and the people.

• Seek the company of the learned and the wise in search of solving the problems of your country and the righteousness of your people.

• No good can come in keeping silent as to government or in speaking out of ignorance.

• The righteous are men of virtue, whose logic is straightforward, whose dress is unostentatious, whose path is modest, whose actions are many and who are undeterred by difficulties.

• Choose the best among your people to administer justice among them. Choose someone who does not easily give up, who is unruffled by enmities, someone who will not persist in wrongdoing, who will not hesitate to pursue right once he knows it, someone whose heart knows no greed, who will not be satisfied with a minimum of explanation without seeking the maximum of understanding, who will be the most steadfast when doubt is cast, who will be the least impatient in correcting the opponent, the most patient in pursuing the truth, the most stern in meting out judgment; someone who is unaffected by flattery and not swayed by temptation and these are but few.

Source: Nahg El Balagha, interpreted by Imam Mohammad Abdou, Part I, Dar El Balagha, second edition, Beirut, 1985.

Imam Ali's Words on Governance

Adaptations from the words of Imam Ali in the Arab Fund for Economic and Social Development, United Nations Development Program (English version).

Martyrs of Shilkarpur

A group of martyrs that were killed in a terrorist attack on a mosque in Shikarpur, Pakistan.

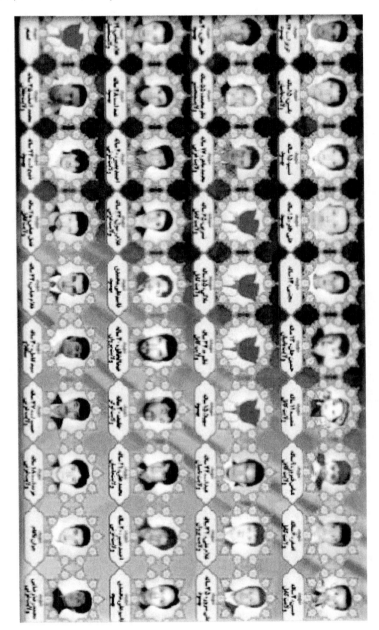

Martyrs in Kabul

A group of victims of the terrorist operation on the Day of Ashura in Kabul in 1433 AH (December 2011).

The Author in Afghanistan

The author visiting a mass grave of Shiite civilians killed at by Taliban terrorists in the area of Gibreel Harat in Afghanistan in the year 1421 AH / 2001 AD.

Printed in Great Britain
by Amazon

83415457R00132